NOTES FROM THE GALLOWS

NOTES
FROM THE
GALLOWS

JULIUS FUCHIK

INTRODUCTION BY SAMUEL SILLEN

PEREGRINE SMITH BOOKS
SALT LAKE CITY

Copyright 1948 by New Century Publishers, Inc.

This facsimile edition is a Peregrine Smith Book, published by
Gibbs Smith, Publisher
P.O. Box 667
Layton, UT 84041

Cover design by Clane Graves

Manufactured in the United States of America

95 94 93 92 91 90   9 8 7 6 5 4 3 2 1

Library of Congress Cataloging-in-Publication Data

Fučík, Julius, 1903-1943.
[Reportáž psaná na oprátce. English]
Notes from the gallows/Julius Fuchik; preface by Samuel Sillen. p. cm.
Translation of: Reportáž psaná na oprátce.
Reprint. Originally published: New York: New Century Publishers, 1948.
ISBN 0-87905-252-X
1. Fučík, Julius, 1903-1943. 2. World War, 1939-1945—Prisoners and prisons,
German. 3. World War, 1939-45—Personal narratives,
Czech. 4. Journalists—Czechoslovakia—Biography. 5. Communists-
Czechoslovakia—Biography. I. Title.
DB2191.F93A313   1990
940.54 '7243—dc20   90-33737
                                                                            CIP

The paper used in this publication meets the minimum requirements of American
National Standard for Information Sciences—Permanence of Paper for Printed
Library Materials, ANSI Z39.48-1984 ♾

CONTENTS

⎪▌ ⎪▌ ⎪▌

INTRODUCTION

‖ ‖ ‖

JULIUS FUCHIK wrote this book under the shadow of the Nazi hangman's noose. The very form of the manuscript testifies to the invincible courage and resourcefulness of the author. It consists of pencilled slips of paper smuggled one by one, with the aid of a sympathetic Czech guard, from the Gestapo prison at Pankrats, Prague. Fuchik, a man scornful of self-deception, knew he would not live to complete this precarious serial. But he was unyielding in his faith that its "happy ending," as he put it, would soon be written by millions of his own countrymen and by antifascists in other lands.

This confidence in the people and in their future is the root theme of the book. True, we find here, as in so much of the war's prison-literature, an ineffaceable image of fascist cruelty. But this is the picture of one who is not merely a victim of fascism, but also its accuser, judge and moral conqueror. "Oh, what a crop will rise one day from that frightful seeding," he exclaims. And to Fuchik we irresistibly apply the words he chooses to describe a comrade who is "always pointing others into the future, when his own future pointed straight toward death."

Fuchik was killed by the Gestapo, but the future to which he points in this book is a living reality in his native

Czechoslovakia. Indeed, the book itself is the most widely read of all works about the war in that country, and Fuchik is celebrated as one of the great national heroes. The book has also been translated into the tongue of virtually every country that played a part in defeating Hitler, including the Soviet Union, Yugoslavia, and France. Of the Soviet Union, Fuchik once wrote an admiring book entitled *In the Land Where Tomorrow Is Already Yesterday*. The future of which he writes in the present book has already taken shape in Czechoslovakia and the other new democracies of Europe.

A journalist, literary critic and Communist leader, Julius Fuchik was born on February 23, 1903, in Prague-Smichov. His father was a steel worker as well as an amateur actor and singer. Fuchik's own activity in the working class movement and in the cultural world of Czechoslovakia began when he was in his early teens. As a student at the University of Prague, he studied literature, music and art. Earning his living as a worker, he joined the Communist Party, wrote for socialist reviews, and became a leading figure in the Communist Students Organization. In 1929 he became editor-in-chief of *Tvorba* (Creation), which under his leadership was an influential cultural and political review. He subsequently became editor of *Rude Pravo*, organ of the Communist Party of Czechoslovakia.

Following two visits to the Soviet Union, which he reported to his countrymen as correspondent, lecturer, and editor, Fuchik was persecuted and repeatedly imprisoned by Czech reactionaries. At the time of Munich, the Communist press was illegalized, the party driven underground.

With the Nazi occupation, Fuchik went into hiding. He devoted himself to Marxist literary-historical studies and was at the same time instrumental in organizing illegal headquarters for the Party. With his colleagues he published the underground central organ *Rude Pravo* (he was its editor), and other publications including the satirical review *Trnavecek* (The Tiny Whistle).

Of the Communist Party of Czechoslovakia, today the majority party of that country, Fuchik writes in this book with pride and devotion. This party, under savage persecution, proved to be an indestructible part of the strength of the Czech working class and the entire nation. At a time when imperialist reactionaries in America, like the Munichmen of Czechoslovakia, seek to smash the vanguard party of our own working class, it is particularly instructive to read Fuchik's book. Here we see the Communists in their true light as the most determined defenders of the people's interests. Here we see that genuine friendship with the Soviet Union, the land of socialism, is the prerequisite for the defense of any nation against reaction and fascism. It is as a great Czech patriot, as a staunch son of the Czech working class, that Fuchik speaks with respect and love of the Soviet Union.

He was arrested by the Gestapo, tortured, murdered at the age of 40. But in these pages, so magnificently unlabored, so shrewd in observation, so rich in the love of life, Fuchik has left an enduring work of literature. And an enduring lesson—let us remember his last line: "Be on guard!" "In real life," he wrote, "there are no spectators: you all participate in life." Is not this as true of real literature as it is of life? This book is a noble participation in the continuing fight—how much closer now to our own homes!—against the monstrous inhumanities of fascism.

SAMUEL SILLEN

A NOTE

|| || ||

IN THE CONCENTRATION camp at Ravensbrück I heard from a fellow-prisoner that my husband, Julius Fuchik, was condemned to death by a Nazi court in Berlin on August 25, 1943.

Questions about his further fate merely echoed back from the high walls around the camp.

After the defeat of Hitler Germany in May, 1945, prisoners were released whom the fascists had not had time to torture quite to death. I was among those saved.

Returning to my liberated homeland, I searched for my husband, just as others by the thousand searched and searched for their husbands, wives, children, fathers and mothers, who had been dragged off by the German invaders to numberless torture hells.

I learned that he had been executed in Berlin on September 8, 1943, the fourteenth day after his sentence.

I also learned that Julius Fuchik had written notes while in Pankrats Prison in Prague. It was a Czech guard, A. Kolinsky, who brought paper and a pencil to his cell and secretly carried away the sheets, one by one. I met that guard and finally collected the notes my husband had written in Pankrats Prison. The numbered sheets came from hiding with various faithful people, and are here presented to the reader—the last chapter of Julius Fuchik's life work.

AUGUSTINA FUCHIK

PREFACE

SITTING AT "ATTENTION," your body rigidly erect, your hands gripping your knees, eyes riveted on the yellowing wall of a room in the former Petchek bank building—this is certainly not a position conducive to meditation. But who can force your thoughts to sit at attention?

We shall never know who or when, but someone once called this hall in Petchek building "the Cinema." The Germans called it "domestic imprisonment," but "Cinema" was a stroke of genius. The spacious hall contained six long rows of benches, occupied by the rigid bodies of those under investigation. The bare wall before their staring eyes became a screen on which they projected more scenes than have ever been filmed, as they waited to be called to another hearing, to torture, to death. The film of one's whole life or of some minor moment of life, a film of one's mother, wife or children, of one's broken home or ruined life. Films of courageous comrades—or of betrayal. The film of the man to whom I gave that anti-Nazi leaflet, of blood which is flowing again, of a firm grip of the hand which held me loyal. Films full of horror or of brave decision, of hate or love, fear and hope. Our backs turned to life, each of us died here daily before his own eyes. But not all were reborn.

I have seen the film of my life a hundred times, thousands

of details. Now I shall attempt to set it down. If the hangman's noose strangles before I finish, millions remain to write its "happy ending."

J. F.

Written in the
Gestapo prison at Pankrats, Prague
in the spring, 1943

Chapter I

TWENTY-FOUR HOURS

IN FIVE MINUTES the clock will strike ten. A beautiful, warm spring evening, April 24, 1942.

I am hurrying as fast as I can while pretending to be an elderly man with a limp—hurrying to reach the Jelineks' before the building is closed at curfew, at ten. There my "adjutant" Mirek is waiting. I know that he has nothing important to tell me this time, nor I to tell him. But to miss an appointed meeting might cause panic, and I should hate to cause extra worry for those two fine souls, my hosts.

They greet me with a cup of tea. Mirek is there—and the Fried couple, also. That is an unnecessary risk. "I like to see you, comrades, but not together this way. So many in one room at once is the best way to jail, to death. You will either have to stick to the rules of conspiracy, or quit working with us, for you are endangering yourselves and others. Do you understand?"

"We understand."

"And what have you brought me?"

"Copy for the May first number of *Red Rights.*"

"Excellent. And you, Mirko?"

"There's nothing new. The work is going well . . ."

"That's all. See you after the first of May. I'll send a message. So long."

"Another cup of tea, chief."

"No, no, Mrs. Jelinek. There are too many of us here."

"At least one cup, please."

Steam rises from the fresh-poured tea.

Someone rings at the door.

At this time of night? Who can it be?

The visitors are impatient. They bang on the door.

"Open up! The police!"

Quick through the window. Escape. I have a pistol; I'll hold them back. Too late. Gestapo men under the windows, aiming pistols into the room. Detectives have forced the door, rush into the room through the kitchen. One, two, three—nine of them. They do not see me because I am behind the door through which they came. I could easily shoot them in the back. But their nine pistols point at the two women and three unarmed men. If I fire, my five friends will fall before I do. If I shoot myself, there will be shooting anyway, and those five will die. If I don't shoot, they will sit in jail six months or a year, and the revolution will set them free, alive. Only Mirek and I will not come out alive; they will torture us. They won't get anything out of me, but out of Mirek? A man who fought in Spain, a man who lived through two years of concentration camp in France, who came from France back to Prague illegally in the midst of war—no, he will never tell. I have two seconds to decide. Or is it three seconds?

If I shoot, I don't save anyone, except myself from torture —but I sacrifice the lives of five comrades. Is that true? Yes.

So it is decided. I step out of the corner.

"Ah, one more!"

[2]

The first blow in my face. Hard enough to knock a man out.

"Hands up."

Another punch, and another.

This is just as I imagined it would be.

The orderly apartment is now a pile of furniture and broken things.

More blows and kicks.

"March."

They drag me into an automobile. Pistols always pointing at me. They start on me in the car.

"Who are you?"

"Professor Horak."

"You lie."

I shrug my shoulders.

"Sit still or we shoot!"

"Well, shoot."

Instead, they punch me.

We pass a streetcar. It looks to me as though it were draped with white. A wedding car—at night? I must be feverish.

The Petchek building, Gestapo headquarters. I never thought I should enter here alive. They make me run up to the fourth floor. Aha, the famous II-A section, anti-Communist investigation. I seem to be almost curious.

A tall thin commissar in charge of the arrest unit puts a revolver in his pocket and takes me into his office. He lights my cigarette.

"Who are you?"

"Professor Horak."

"You lie."

The watch on his wrist shows eleven o'clock.

"Search him."

They strip me and search.

"He has an identity card."

"The name?"

"Professor Horak."

"Check up on that."

They telephone.

"Of course, he is not registered. The card is forged."

"Who gave it to you?"

"Police headquarters."

Then the first blow with a stick. The second, third . . . shall I count them? No, my boy, there is nowhere to report such statistics.

"Your name? Speak. Your address? Speak. With whom did you have contact? Speak. Their addresses? Talk! Talk! Talk, or we'll beat you."

How many blows can a man stand?

The radio squeaks midnight. The cafes must be closing, the last guests going home. Lovers stand before house doors unable to take leave of each other. The tall thin commissar comes into the room with a cheerful smile.

"Everything in order, Mr. Editor?"

Who told them that? The Jelineks? The Frieds? Why, they don't even know my name.

"You see, we know everything. Talk! Be reasonable."

In their special dictionary to be reasonable means to betray.

I won't be reasonable.

[4]

"Tie him up and give him some more."

One o'clock. The last streetcars are pulling in, streets are empty, the radio says good night to its last faithful listeners.

"Who else is a member of the Central Committee? Where are your transmitters? Where is your printing shop? Talk! Talk! Talk!"

By now I can count the blows again. The only pain I feel is in the lips I have been biting.

"Off with his boots."

That is true, my feet have not yet been beaten numb. I feel that. Five, six, seven—as though that stick shot up to my brain each time.

Two o'clock. Prague is asleep. Somewhere a child will whimper, a man will pat his wife on the hips.

"Talk! Talk!"

My tongue feels along my bleeding gums and tries to count how many teeth have been knocked out. I can't keep count. Twelve, fifteen, seventeen? No, that is the number of commissars conducting my "hearing." Some of them are visibly tired. But death still does not come.

Three o'clock. Early morning moves in from the suburbs. Truck-gardeners drive toward their markets, street-sweepers go out to work. Perhaps I shall live to see one more day break.

They bring in my wife.

"Do you know him?"

I swallow the blood from around my mouth so that she will not see . . . but that is foolish because blood oozes from every inch of my face and from my finger tips.

"Do you know him?"

"No, I don't."

She said it without betraying her terror by even a glance. Pure gold. She kept our pledge never to recognize me, although it is almost unnecessary now. Who was it gave them my name?

They led her away. I said farewell with the most cheerful glance I could summon. Perhaps it wasn't cheerful. I don't know.

Four o'clock. Is dawn breaking or not? The darkened windows give no answer. And death is slow in coming. Shall I go to meet it? How?

I strike back at someone and fall to the floor. They kick me. Stamp on me with their boots. That's it, now the end will come quickly. The black commissar pulls me up by the beard and shows me a handful of torn out whiskers with a devilish laugh. It really is comical, and I don't feel pain any longer.

Five o'clock—six—seven—ten. Then it is noon, the workmen are at their benches, children are in school. People buy and sell in the shops, at home they are getting lunch. Perhaps mother is thinking of me this moment, perhaps my comrades know that I was arrested and have taken precautions against being caught themselves . . . what if I should talk . . . no, I never will, you can count on me, truly. Anyway the end can't be far off now. This is all a nightmare, a horrible feverish nightmare. Blows all over me, then they throw water on me to bring me back. Then more blows, and shouts. "Talk! Talk! TALK!" But I still can't die. Mother, Dad, why did you make me so strong as to stand this?

[6]

Afternoon. Five o'clock. They are all tired out by this time. Their blows come slower, at long intervals, kept up out of inertia. Suddenly from a distance, from an immeasurable distance, comes a calm quiet voice, as kind as a pat:

"*Er hat schon genug.* He has had enough."

Some time after that I was sitting at a table, which kept falling away and then coming back to me. Some one came in and gave me water. Somebody offered me a cigarette, which I couldn't lift. Now someone tries to put on my slippers, but says he can't. Then they half lead and half carry me down stairs into an auto. As we drive someone covers me with his pistol, which seems laughable, in my condition. We pass a streetcar, garlanded with white flowers, a wedding car—but maybe that is just a dream. Either a dream or fever, or dying—or death itself. But dying is hard, and this is easy—or it isn't either hard or easy. This is light as down—if you take a breath you will blow it all away.

All away? No, not yet. Now I am standing again, really standing alone, without any support. Just before my face is a dirty yellow wall, splashed . . . with what? With blood, it looks like. . . . Yes, it is blood. I raise a finger and smear it . . . yes, it is fresh . . . it is my blood . . .

Someone behind hits me on the head and orders me to raise my arms and bend my knees to a squat. Down—up—down. The third time I fall over . . .

A tall SS-man stands over me, kicking me to get up. It is quite useless to kick. Someone else washes my face, I am sitting at a table. A woman gives me some sort of medicine and asks where it hurts worst. I say all the pain seems to be in my heart.

[7]

"You have no heart," says the tall SS-man.

"Oh, I certainly have," I say, and am suddenly proud that I have strength left to stand up for my heart.

Again everything vanishes—the wall, the woman with the medicine and the tall SS.

When I come to, the door of a cell opens before me. A fat SS-man drags me inside, pulls off the shreds of my shirt, lays me on the straw mattress. He feels my swollen body over and orders compresses.

"Just look," he says to the second man and wags his head. "Look what a thorough job they do."

Again from a distance, an immeasurable distance, I hear that calm quiet voice, as kind as a pat:

"He can't last till morning."

In five minutes it will strike ten. On a beautiful warm spring evening, April 25, 1942.

Chapter II

DYING

*When the warmth of the sun and light of the stars
Disappear for us, disappear for us . . .*

Two MEN, their hands folded downward in prayer, pace
slowly one behind the other round and round in a white-
walled crypt. Their untrained voices drag out a sad dirge.

*. . . how pleasantly the soul wings its way
To heaven above, to heaven above . . .*

Someone has died. Who? I try to turn my head to get a
look at the coffin and corpse, with the two candles pointing
upward by his head.

*. . . where night is no more,
Where eternal is the light of day . . .*

I succeed in raising my eyes and rolling them about. There
is no one else here. I can't see anyone but those two—and
myself. For whom are they singing that dirge?

*. . . where the eternal star blazes,
Jesus Himself, Jesus Himself.*

This is a funeral. It certainly seems like a funeral, but whom
are they burying? Let's see who is here—only those two
and I. And I! Then it is my funeral? But listen, men, there

is some mistake. I'm not dead. I'm still alive. Can't you see me looking at you, talking to you? Stop. Don't bury me yet!

> *. . . when someone gives us his last farewell,*
> *His last farewell . . .*

They don't hear. Are they deaf? Don't I talk loud enough? Or am I really dead perhaps, and they unable to hear a voice without a body? Is my body to lie here on its face while I watch my own funeral? Comical.

> *. . . he turns his fervent eyes*
> *To heaven above, to heaven above . . .*

Now I remember. Someone struggled to raise me up and dress me. Then they carried me on a pall, their hob-nailed boots ringing in the corridor. And then . . . That is all. I don't remember any more.

> *. . . where the eternal light stays ever.*

But this is all absurd. I am still alive. I feel only some distant pain and thirst. The dead aren't thirsty. I put all my strength into an attempt to move my hand, and a strange, unnatural voice bursts out of me:

"Water!"

At last! The two men stop walking in a circle. Now they lean over me, one of them lifts my head and holds a pitcher of water to my lips.

"Boy, you must eat something, too. For two days you have had only water."

What's that he tells me? Two days already? What day is it today?

[10]

"Monday."

Monday. And Friday I was arrested. Oh, how heavy my head is. And the water so cool. Sleep. Let me sleep. A drop has stirred the surface of the spring. The spring on the meadow among the hills I know, near the forester's house under Roklan Mountain, and a light endless drizzle sings in the needles of the trees . . . how sweet it is to sleep . . .

. . . And when I wake up again it is Tuesday evening, and over me leans a dog. A wolf-dog. He looks at me searchingly with his beautiful wise eyes and asks:

"Where did you live?"

Oh, no, it's not the dog. The voice is somebody else's. Yes, there is somebody else standing there. I see high boots, another pair of high boots, one more pair of high boots and the pants of a soldier. I can't see higher, my head is dizzy as soon as I try to lift it. Oh, who cares, let me sleep . . .

Wednesday.

The two men who had sung the psalms now sit at the table eating out of an earthen bowl. Now I can tell them apart. One is younger than the other, and it seems they are not monks. This is no monastery cell but a prison cell. The planks on the floor run together away from my eyes and there, at the end, there is a heavy sinister door . . .

A key grates in the lock, the two men jump up and stand at attention. Two other men in uniforms of the SS enter and order them to dress me. I did not know how much pain is hidden in each sock, in each sleeve. They lay me on a stretcher and carry me down the stairs, their heavy boots thundering in the long corridor . . . this then is the way they carried me once before when I finally lost consciousness. Where does it lead? In what hell does it end?

In the shadowy, unfriendly reception office of the police prison of Pankrats. They place me on the floor and a Czech voice, faking friendliness, translates the angry question of a German voice:

"Do you know her?"

I lift my chin with my hand. Facing the stretcher stands a young girl with a broad face. She stands proudly erect, head up, not sullen, but noble. Only her eyes look downward, just enough to see me and to greet me.

"I don't know her."

I remember I saw her just once, perhaps for a second in that wild night in the Petchek building. This is the second time. And alas, never for a third time, to press her hand for the loftiness with which she now stood here. She was the wife of Arnošt Lorenz. She was executed in the first days of martial law in 1942.

"But this one you certainly know."

Anichka Jirásková! For heaven's sake, Anichka, how come you are here? I did not tell your name, you had nothing to do with me. I do not know you, understand, I do not know you.

"I don't know her."

"Be sensible, man!"

"I don't know her."

"Julo, it doesn't matter," Anichka says, and a slight movement of her fingers twisting her handkerchief betrays her excitement. "It doesn't matter. Somebody identified me."

"Who?"

"Shut up!" They prevent her answering and push her violently aside as she leans over me and stretches out her hand.

Anichka!

I no longer hear their questions. Painlessly, as though I were an onlooker at a distance, I feel two SS-men carrying me back to the cell. How brutally they jounce the stretcher, and laughingly ask me whether I would prefer to hang from a rope.

Thursday.

I begin to perceive things again. One of my fellow prisoners, the younger one, is called Karek and he calls the older one "father." They tell me something about themselves, but it's all confused in my head. There seems to be a mine in their talk, and some children sitting on benches. I hear a bell, there is probably a fire somewhere. Every day, they say, a doctor comes to see me and an SS orderly—it's not so bad with me after all and soon, they say, I shall be all right again. That's what the "father" says and he says it so convincingly, and Karek backs him so ardently, that even in my misery I feel they are telling a white lie. Nice fellows! I am sorry I cannot believe them.

Afternoon.

The door of the cell opens and quietly, on tiptoe, the dog enters. He stops at my head and again looks searchingly at me. Again two pair of heavy boots. I already know one pair belongs to the owner of the dog, the superintendent of Pankrats prison, the second pair to the chief of the anti-Communist section of the Gestapo, who presided at my examination that first night. And there are some civilian

[13]

trousers. My eyes run upward on them—yes, I know, this is the tall thin commissar who led the raiding squad. He sits down on a chair and begins the questioning.

"You lost your game. Save yourself at least. Talk!"

He offers me a cigarette. I don't want it. I couldn't bear it.

"How long did you live with the Baxas?"

With the Baxas. That's too much. Who told them?

"Now, you see, we know everything. Speak up!"

If you know everything, why should I tell you any more? I have not wasted my life, and I will not spoil the end of it.

The investigation lasts one hour. He does not shout; patiently he repeats his questions and when no answer is forthcoming, he asks another one and another, without end.

"Don't you understand? This is the end, you know. You have lost your game."

"It is only I who have lost out."

"You still believe in the victory of the Commune?"

"Naturally."

"He still believes?" asks the chief in German—and the tall commissar translates—"he still believes in the victory of Russia?"

"Naturally. It can't be otherwise."

I am tired. I had gathered all my strength to be on guard; now consciousness is vanishing quickly as blood flowing from a deep wound. I feel them stretch out their hands—probably reading the sign of death on my forehead. In some countries it is even customary for the executioner to kiss the condemned before he carries out the verdict.

Evening.

Two men with folded hands walk in a circle, one behind

[14]

the other, and sing a sad psalm with wailing uneven voices:

When the warmth of the sun and the light of the stars
Disappear for us, disappear for us. . . .

Oh good people, stop it! Maybe it's a nice song, but today, today is the eve of the First of May, of the most beautiful, most joyful holiday of man. I try to sing something cheerful, but perhpas it sounds even sadder because young Karek turns away and the "father" wipes his eyes. Who cares, I continue singing, and they join me slowly. I fall asleep in a happy mood.

The early morning of May First.

The clock in the tower of the prison strikes three. For the first time I hear it clearly. I have regained full consciousness. I feel the fresh air pouring down through the open window and flowing around my straw mattress on the floor. I suddenly feel the stalks of straw. It is hard to breathe, for every spot of my body has a thousand pains. Suddenly, as if you open a window, I see clearly that this is the end. I am dying.

It took you a long time to come, Death. Once I hoped it would be many, many years before I made your acquaintance. I hoped to live the life of a free man, to work a lot and to love a lot, to sing and to wander about the world. I had only come to maturity and still had a great deal of strength. I do not have it any longer. It is vanishing.

I loved life and for its beauty I went out to fight. I loved you, people, and was happy when you returned my love. I suffered when you misunderstood me. You, whomever I wronged, forgive me; you whom I cheered, forget. May sad-

[15]

ness never belong to my name. This is my last will for you, father and mother, sisters, for you, my Gusta, for you, comrades, for all those whom I loved. If you think tears can clear away the sad dust of grief, weep for a while. But do not regret. I lived for joy; I am dying for joy and it would be an injustice to place upon my grave an angel of sorrow.

First of May! In these morning hours we rose in the suburbs and prepared our flags. In these hours on the streets of Moscow the first ranks took their places for the May Day parade. In these hours today millions of people are fighting the last battle for the freedom of men, and thousands die in the struggle. I am one of them. And to be one of them is beautiful, one of the soldiers of the last battle.

But dying is not beautiful. I am choking. I cannot breathe. I hear the rattling in my throat, I might wake up my fellow prisoners. Maybe, if I drank some water. . . . But all the water in the pitcher is gone. Just six steps from me, though, in the toilet in the corner of the cell, there is plenty of water. Will I have strength enough to get to it?

I crawl on my belly, quietly, oh so quietly—as though all the glory of death depended on my not waking anyone. I get there finally, and drink the water greedily out of the toilet.

I do not know how long it took, I do not know how long I crawled back. Consciousness is vanishing again. I search for the pulse in my wrist, and cannot feel anything. My heart bounds high into my throat, and falls suddenly back. I fall with it, fall a long time. Midway I hear Karek's voice.

"Father, father, do you hear? The poor fellow is breathing his last."

In the morning the doctor came.

But of all that I learned much later.

He came, examined me and shook his head. Then he returned to the infirmary, tore up the report of death which he had filled out the evening before with my name on it and said with the self-assurance of an expert:

"He has the constitution of a horse."

Chapter III

CELL 267

SEVEN STEPS from the door to the window, seven steps from the window to the door.

I know that thoroughly.

How many times have I paced that distance on the pine boards of my Pankrats cell! Perhaps I sat in that cell just because I saw too clearly the results for the Czech nation of the ruinous policies of our city folk. My nation is now being stretched upon the cross; before my cell pace German guards and somewhere out there the political Fates spin the threads of treason. How many centuries do men need to open their eyes? How many thousand prison-cells has humanity plodded through on the road forward? And how many more must it go through? Oh, Neruda's Christ-child, there is no end to man's road to salvation. But man is awake at last, awake at last.

Seven paces there, seven paces back. Along one wall a folding bunk, on the other a dreary brown shelf with its earthenware bowl. Yes, I know all that. Prisons are mechanized now, with central heating, a flush toilet in place of the old bucket—and the people are mechanized also. Chiefly the people—mere automatons. Press a button and a key grates in the lock of the door, or the peep-hole opens into the cell—the prisoners jump up no matter what they are do-

[18]

ing, stand at attention one behind the other. As the door opens, the eldest in the cell must shout in one breath:

"Attention! Cell two-hundred-sixty-seven occupied by three men—everything in order."

Number 267 is our cell, but the automatons do not operate quite precisely today. Only two jump up. I lie still on my straw mattress under the window—have been lying on my face a week, two weeks, a month, six weeks. I am just being reborn. I can already turn my head, raise my hand. I have raised myself on one elbow, even tried to turn over on my back. But I can certainly write it quicker than I could do it then.

There have been changes in the cell. Instead of three names on the door, there are only two, for Karek has disappeared, the younger of the two men who sang that dirge at my funeral. All he left behind are memories of a kind heart. I can see him only in half-dreams, and remember only the last two days of his stay with us. He kept repeating over and over again the details of his case, and I always fell asleep in the middle of his story.

He is named Karek Maletz, a mechanic who worked at the cage of an iron-mine somewhere near Hudlitz. He carried away explosives which were needed in the underground battle. He was arrested nearly two years ago and is going to trial, perhaps in Berlin. There is a whole group going, and who knows what the sentence will be? He has a wife and two children, whom he loves, loves dearly—but . . . it was my duty, you see, I couldn't do anything else.

He used to sit on my bunk and try to make me eat. I couldn't. On Saturday—have I been here eight days?—he tries his most desperate trick and reports to the police-master that I haven't eaten a thing in all the time I have been here. The police-master, that eternally worried Pankrats orderly in an SS uniform without whose permission the Czech doctor cannot even prescribe aspirin, brings in a mug of infirmary soup and stands over me until I down it. Karek is well satisfied with the success of his appeal to force, and the next day pours a mug of Sunday soup into me himself.

But I can't take more. My lacerated gums can't chew even the overboiled potato in our Sunday goulash, my swollen throat refuses to swallow the smallest lump.

"Not even goulash; he doesn't want even goulash," Karek complains, and wags his head sadly over me.

Then he gulps down half my dinner, after dividing fairly with "dad."

Oh, you who did not live through 1942 in Pankrats don't know what goulash tastes like. You can never know! In those worst days, when our stomachs growled with hunger, when the figures under the weekly showers were skeletons covered with human skin, when your best pal stole your food at least with his eyes. Even the disgusting gruel of dehydrated vegetables and diluted tomato sauce seemed a delicacy. In those worst days the trusty dipped a ladle of potatoes into our bowls twice a week, on Thursdays and Sundays, and poured on them a spoonful of goulash gravy with a few shreds of meat. It tasted miraculous—but more than the taste, it was a material reminder of human life, something civilized, something from normal life in the midst of the cruel abnormality of Gestapo imprisonment. We talked about it with sweet rapture. Oh, who can understand the heights of human value a spoonful of good gravy can attain when seasoned with daily dread of dying!

After two months had passed I also understood Karek's consternation when I refused goulash. Nothing was clearer proof of my approaching death than the one fact that I didn't even want to eat goulash.

The night after that they awoke Karek at two o'clock. He had to be ready to leave in five minutes, as though he were just going out for a moment instead of starting on a journey to the end of life, to another prison, concentration camp or the gallows—who knows where? He took time to kneel by my bunk, put his arms around my head and kiss it. Then the raw shout of the uniformed flunky sounded in the corridor saying that there is no place in Pankrats for sentiment. Karek ran out of the door, the lock snapped . . . and we were only two in the cell.

Will we ever meet again, boy? And who will leave next? Which of us two will go first? Where to? Who will come for him? The flunky in an SS uniform—or Death who wears no uniform?

I write now in the echoes of the thoughts which gripped us after that first farewell in prison. A year has passed since then, and the thoughts which followed our pal out the door have been repeated often, with greater poignancy or less. The two names on the door of our cell rose to three, and then only two again—then three, two, three, two—as new prisoners joined us and then departed. Only the two who remained in cell 267 still sit here faithfully:

"Dad" and I.

[21]

"Dad" is a sixty-year-old teacher named Joseph Peshek, senior of the arrested teachers. He was taken eighty-five days before me, because he committed "intrigue against the German Reich" by working on a plan for improving Czech schools after they should be free again.

"Dad" is. . . .

But how can you ever write it all down, my boy? Quite a job to describe two men in one cell for a year. In that time the quote marks around his name "Dad" disappeared; in that time two prisoners of different ages really became father and son. In that time we each accepted favorite expressions from the other's speech, habitual gestures, and even tones of voice. You could not tell today which of the personal property in the cell is his and which is mine, what he brought in with him and what I brought.

He sat up night after night with me, and with his white wet compress cloths scared off death whenever he approached. He cleaned the pus from my wounds and never showed that he was affected by their horrid odor which hung over my bunk. He washed and mended the shreds of my shirt, and when he could no longer hold it together, put one of his own on me. He brought me a tiny daisy and a few blades of grass, which he picked at the risk of his life in the half-hour exercise period one morning in the prison court-yard. His kind eyes followed me out of the cell each time they took me to another "hearing," and he tenderly wrapped my new wounds in wet compresses when I returned. When they took me off at night, he never slept till they had brought me back and he had laid me on the bunk and tucked in my blanket.

That is the way our relationship began after that first night grilling and nothing spoiled it after I could stand up again and begin to repay my filial debts.

But you can never write it all out, my boy, at one sitting. Cell 267 had a rich life that year, and Dad lived through every bit of it in his own way. But the tale is not yet done —and that has the sound of hope.

Cell 267 had a rich life. At times the door opened and we were inspected every hour. That was due to orders for closer supervision over their Communist criminal, but it was also caused by simple curiosity. People often died here when they were not supposed to, but it did not often happen that someone remained alive when everyone expected him to die. Guards came in from other corridors, talking loudly or silently lifting my blanket, expertly savored my wounds and then, according to their natures, either made cynical jokes or adopted a slightly more friendly tone. One of them, whom we called Smarty, comes more often than the others and with a broad smile asks if "that red devil" wants anything. No thank you, nothing. After a few days Smarty discovers that the red devil does need something—a shave. So he brings in the barber.

The barber is the first prisoner from outside our own cell with whom we get acquainted—comrade Bochek. Smarty's well-intentioned kindness turns out to be rather cruel. Dad holds my head while Bochek kneels by the bunk and hacks his way through the undergrowth with a very dull razor blade. His hands tremble and his eyes fill with tears, for he is convinced he is shaving a corpse. I reassure him.

[23]

"Courage, boy. If I lived through that grilling in Petchek Building, I can stand your shaving."

But we are both so weak that we have to stop and rest, he and I.

Two days later I get acquainted with two more prisoners. The commissar gentlemen in Petchek Building have grown impatient. Every day they sent for me the police-master wrote on the slip "Unfit for transportation." So they order me to be sent regardless. Two prisoners in the uniforms of trusties or "house-men" stop in front of our cell with a stretcher. Dad struggles to get some clothes on me; the trusties lay me on the stretcher and carry me off. One of them is comrade Skorepa, the solicitous dad of the whole corridor. The second is ——, who leans over me when I slip on the stretcher tilting down the stairs, and says, "Hold tight."

Then whispers, "In both senses, hold tight."

This time we don't stop in the reception room. They carry me down a long hall filled with people. It is Thursday and relatives come with clean clothes for their prisoners and carry home the soiled to launder. They stare at our cheerless procession with sympathy in their eyes, which I don't quite like. I raise my hand to my head and clench my fist. Perhaps they will realize it is a salute, perhaps it is a silly gesture. But I haven't strength for more, even for a word.

In the prison court-yard they lay the stretcher in a truck. Two SS men sit with the driver, two SS men stand at my head with their hands on the open pouches of their revolvers, and we drive off. The road is in bad shape. The

[24]

wheels bounce from one hole to another, and within two hundred yards I lose consciousness. It is a comic ride through the streets of Prague—a five-ton truck large enough to carry thirty prisoners burns gasoline for one. Two SS in front and two in the rear, their revolvers and vulturous eyes guarding a corpse for fear it may escape from their clutches.

The hearing could not be held with me unconscious, so they drove me back to Pankrats. The same comedy was repeated next day, only this time I held out till we reached the Petchek Building. But the hearing was not long. Commissar Friedrich touched my body a little carelessly, and they drove me back unconscious again.

There followed days in which I could not doubt that I was still alive. Pain—the twin sister of life—reminded me constantly and very pointedly. All Pankrats learned that by some oversight I was alive and began to send me greetings. By signal tappings on the thick walls, and by the eyes of the trusties who brought in the food.

Only my wife did not know anything about me. Alone in a cell one floor below me and a few numbers farther, she lived in anxiety and hope until a woman from a neighboring cell whispered during the exercise period that I had met my end, succumbed in the cell to wounds from my first grilling. That was such a blow that she circled the courtyard in a daze and didn't even feel the woman-guard's fist in her face, forcing her back into the line of trudging figures which form prison life. What scenes passed before her great, kind eyes as she sat through the day staring at her cell wall, too broken to weep? The next day she heard another rumor, that I was not quite beaten to death, but had hanged myself in the cell to escape my pain.

All the while I twisted on my loathsome bunk, turning to the wall each evening to sing to my Gustina the song she loved best. Why couldn't she hear me, when I put such feeling into it?

She knows today; she can hear that song today—even though she is further away than she was then. By now the guards have grown accustomed to the fact that there is singing in cell 267, and no longer bang on the door for silence.

Cell 267 sings. I have sung all my life and see no reason for stopping at the end of it, when one lives most intensely. And what about Dad Peshek? He is an unusual case, passionately fond of singing. He has no voice, nor musical ear nor memory, but he loves song with a beautiful and devoted love. He finds so much joy in singing that I don't hear it when he slips from tone to tone, and doggedly sings G when your ears long for an A. And so we sing whenever we have a cheerful day, or whenever longing presses down. We sing to accompany a comrade leaving, whom we may never see again. We sing to welcome good news from the eastern front. Sing for joy or to comfort ourselves, as people have sung for ages, and will sing as long as they are people.

There is no life without song, as there is no life without the sun. And we need song here in double measure because the sun cannot reach us. Cell 267 faces to the north and only in the summer months does the setting sun etch the bars of our window on the eastern wall for a few minutes. Those few moments Dad stands leaning against his up-

[26]

turned bunk and gazes at that hasty visit of the sun . . . the saddest sight you will ever see.

The sun! How generously he casts his magic rays, what miracles he works before the very eyes of men! But how few people live in sunlight. He will shine, yes, he will shine for us all one day, and we shall all live in his warming rays. It is wonderful to know that. But I would like to know something incomparably less important—will he shine again for us two?

Our cell is toward the north. Only occasionally, when a summer day is unusually lucky, do we see the sun set. Oh, Dad, how I would like to see the sun rise once more.

Chapter IV

NUMBER 400

RESURRECTION is a rather special event. Extraordinary, beyond description. The world is attractive on a beautiful day, after one has slept well. Resurrection is a day more beautiful than the rest, as though you had slept better than ever before. You thought that you knew the stage of life, but resurrection turns on all the reflectors through clear glass and suddenly shows you the stage in fullest light. You thought that you had seen life pretty clearly, but resurrection holds a telescope to your eye, and a microscope at the same time. It is an event completely spring-like, as spring discovers unsuspected magic in surroundings most familiar.

Even here, where you realize that it is only for a moment. Even if your surroundings are as rich and attractive as a Pankrats cell.

Finally one day they lead you out into the world. One day they call you to a hearing without a stretcher. Although it seems quite impossible to you, it is possible to get there. The corridor has a railing, the stairs have railings; you crawl rather than walk. Down below fellow-prisoners take you in hand and pass you out to the prison bus. There you sit, ten or twelve people in a dark mobile cell. New faces smile at you and you smile back. Someone whispers something, and you don't know who it is; you grip someone's hand and don't know whose. The bus turns sharply into the court of the Petchek Building, your new comrades carry you down. You all walk into a spacious room with bare walls and five rows of benches, on which figures sit at attention. Their hands frozen to their knees, they stare immovable at the empty wall before them . . . that, my boy, is a bit of your new life, called the "Cinema." The screen on which you will review your whole life a hundred times.

MAY INTERLUDE, 1943

This is the first of May 1943, an intermission in which I have a chance to write. What luck!—to be a Communist editor again for a moment, and write a story on the May parade of the battle-strength of the new world.

Don't expect to hear about waving flags, nothing of that kind. Nor can I tell you about any exciting action, which people so like to hear. It was much simpler than that today, no explosive waves of thousands of marchers who poured through the streets of Prague on May 1st in other years. No exquisite sea of millions, which I have seen flood the Red Square in Moscow. You don't see millions, or even hundreds here, only a handful of comrades. And yet you feel that this is not less important, for here is a review of a new force as it passes through the fiercest fire and turns not to ashes, but to steel. A review in the battle trenches, in trenches where we wear field gray.

This test takes place in such minor events that I doubt

[29]

if you, who have not lived through the furnace of battle, can understand it as you read. Perhaps you will understand. Believe me, strength is being born here.

The morning greeting from our neighboring cell taps out two measures from Beethoven. It is more emphatic today, more festive, and the wall speaks in higher tones.

We dress in the best that we have. The same in all the cells.

We have a gala breakfast. The trusties parade before the open cell doors with black coffee, bread and water. Comrade Skorepa hands out three buns instead of two as his May Day greeting. The greeting of a careful soul, who finds some simple act to express his feelings. Our fingers touch under the buns and exchange a pressure ever so slight. One dares not speak—they even watch the expression of our eyes. But the dumb can talk quite clearly with their fingers.

Below our window the women prisoners run out for their setting-up exercises. I climb up on the table to look down through the bars. Perhaps they will look up. They see me, and raise clenched fists in greeting. And again. It is lively down in the court—really cheerful compared to other days. The guard does not see—or perhaps doesn't wish to see. Even that is a part of the May Day parade.

Then comes our period, and I am to lead the exercises. It is the first of May, boys, let's begin with something new, whether the guard is looking or not. First exercise is swinging the sledge-hammer—one, two, one, two. Second comes cutting grain. The hammer and sickle—the men begin to understand. A smile goes down the ranks and they bend to the exercises with a vigor. This is our May Day demonstration, boys, this pantomine is our May Day oath that we shall stand firm, even we who march toward death.

Back to the cells. Nine o'clock. The clock tower in the Kremlin is striking ten and the parade starts across the Red Square. Come along, Dad, they are singing the International. The International sounds around the world; let it ring out in our cell, too. We sing it, and one revolutionary song follows another. We don't want to be lonely—nor are we alone. We belong to those who dare sing freely out in the world. They are in battle, just as we. . . .

> *Comrades in the prisons*
> *Behind those frigid walls,*
> *You're with us, you're with us*
> *Though you can't march in our ranks.*

Yes, we're with you.

In cell 267 we thought that a fitting close to our May Day celebration, 1943. But it was not the end. The trusty from the women's corridor is strolling out in the court-yard whistling the March of the Red Army. Then she whistles *Partizanka* and other Soviet songs, adding her courage to that in the men's cells. And the man in the uniform of the Czech police, who brought me paper and pencil and stands guard outside my door so no one can surprise me while I write. And the other Czech guard who started me at this writing and carries the sheets away to be hidden until the right time for them to appear in print. He could pay with his very head for this piece of paper, and risks his life to build a paper bridge between today behind the bars and

[31]

tomorrow in liberty. They are all fighting the one battle, fighting courageously, wherever they are placed, with whatever weapons come to hand. They are so simple about it, so unostentatious and utterly without pathos that you would never realize this is a battle to the death, in which it is still nip and tuck whether they win or lose their lives.

Ten times, twenty times you have seen the soldiers of the revolution parade on May Day, and it was grand. But only in battle can you see the real strength of this army, and realize that it is invincible. Death is simpler than you thought, and heroism has no halo round its head. But the battle is crueler than you supposed, and it takes immeasurable strength to hold out and win through to victory. You see this army move, but don't always realize what strength it has. Its blows are so simple and logical.

Today you realize it.

At the May Day parade of 1943.

May First, 1943, interrupted for a moment the flow of this tale. That is as it should be. On festive days one thinks differently, and the joy I feel today may distort my memory of it.

But the "Cinema" in the Petchek Building was certainly nothing pleasant. It is the entry hall of the torture chamber, from which you hear the shrieks and moans of others and wonder what you will have to face. You see people go in strong and healthy; they return two or three hours later broken and crippled in the grilling. A strong voice bids you goodbye as it enters—and returns choked with pain, broken and feverish. Sometimes you see what is even worse. You see a person go in with clear direct eyes; but when he returns he dares not look you in the face. He met a moment of weakness up there in the inquisition room, just a moment of indecision, of fear, of an overpowering wish to save himself. That means that tomorrow they will bring in new victims who must begin to live through all the horror from the beginning, people whom that comrade betrayed to the enemy.

The sight of someone who has lost his courage and his conscience is worse than the sight of one whose body has been crippled. If your eyes have been wiped by death, who stalks through here, if your senses have been stimulated by resurrection, you know without words who has wavered, who has betrayed another, who has harbored for a moment the thought that it would be better to break down and tell about the least important of his fellow-workers. Those who weaken are pitiful. What kind of life will they have, paid for with the life of a comrade!

That may not have been the thought which passed through my mind the first time I sat in the Cinema, but it returned to me there very often. It appeared that morning in different surroundings, in the room which is the well of understanding, in Number 400.

I had not sat long in the Cinema, perhaps an hour, perhaps an hour and a half, when a voice called my name from behind my back. Two civilians speaking Czech took charge of me, put me in the elevator, got out on the fourth floor and led me into another spacious room with the number 400 on the door.

At first I sat off by myself, quite alone on a solitary chair in the back near the wall, and glanced around with the strange feeling of a person who imagines that he lived once before through the moment which is passing just now. Have I ever been here before? No, never. But it is all familiar. I know this room, have dreamed a cruel feverish dream about it, which distorted and made it disgustingly repulsive, and yet did not render it unrecognizable. Just now it is attractive, full of daylight and clear colors, Tyn Church and the green park of Letna and the Castle visible through the large windows and their light grills. In my dream it was dark and windowless, with a dusty yellow color, which made people look like shadows. Yes, there were people here. Now it is empty, and the six benches close behind each other form a bright yellow meadow of dandelions and buttercups. In the dream it was full of people, sitting next to each other on the benches, their faces pale and bloody. There, quite near the door, stood a man with tortured eyes, in blue working clothes, longing to drink, to drink, and then collapsed on the floor like a falling curtain. . . .

Yes, that is how it was, but I now realize that it was not a dream. That delirious dream had actually happened.

It was on that night of my arrest and first hearing. They brought me here three times—perhaps ten times, how do I know—whenever they wished to rest or to work on someone else. I was barefoot and remember how pleasantly the tile floor cooled my swollen feet.

The benches that night were full of workmen from the Junkers plant, the Gestapo catch for that evening. The man in the blue overalls by the door was comrade Barton of the party cell at Junkers, the indirect cause of my arrest. In order that no one be held responsible for my fate, I must say that it was not due to the cowardice or treason of any of the comrades, but merely to carelessness and bad luck. Comrade Barton was trying to make contact for his cell with people higher up in the resistance movement. His friend, Comrade Jelinek, broke underground rules by promising to make the contact for him without first asking me to make contact direct, from the top down. That was one mistake. The second was that a spy named Dvorak got next to comrade Barton, and learned the name of Jelinek. Thus the Jelinek family fell into Gestapo clutches, not by failing in any major assignment—which they had been carrying out faithfully for two years—but for that little service which was a step out of line with the rules of conspiracy. It happened that they decided at the Petchek Building to arrest the Jelineks that very evening when I visited them, and that they came in such force purely by accident. It had not been planned that way; the Jelineks were to have been arrested the following day. But after their success in rounding up the Junkers cell members, the Gestapo unit exuberantly went for the Jelineks just for a lark. Our surprise at their visit was no greater than theirs at finding me there. They didn't even know whom they had caught. And perhaps they would never have found out except that at the same time they. . . .

It was a long while before I had a chance to continue this first meditation in Number 400. By that time I was not alone, the benches had filled and a line stood around the walls as the hours raced on full of surprises. Some surprises were so queer I couldn't understand them; others were vicious, and those I understod all too well.

The first surprise was neither strange nor vicious, but

[35]

kind, very small and unimportant, and yet I shall never forget it. The Gestapo agent who was watching me—I recall he was the one who turned all my pockets inside out after my arrest—tossed me a half a burning cigarette. The first cigarette in three weeks, the first cigarette for a man who had returned to earth a second time. Should I pick it up? Or will he think he has bought me with a cigarette? But the glance with which he follows the cigarette is completely frank; he is not interested in buying anybody. Still I couldn't smoke it to the end. New-born babies are not strong smokers.

The second surprise—four men goose-step into the room and greet those present in Czech, including me. They sit down behind the table, lay out their papers, light cigarettes, quite comfortably, as though they were mere officials. But I know them, I know at least three of them—is it possible that they are in the service of the Gestapo? Perhaps so—but even these three? Why, that is Teringl or Renek, as we called him, a long-time secretary of the union and party, slightly wild by nature, but loyal. That is impossible! That one is Anka Vikova, still erect and still pretty, even though her hair is entirely white. She was a hard, determined fighter—no, this is impossible! And that one is Vashek Rezek, bricklayer from the north Bohemian mines and then district secretary of the party—sure, I know him. After all the struggles we went through together in the north, how could anything break his back? No, impossible! But what are they doing here? What do they want?

I had not found answers to these questions, when the others appeared. They brought in Mirka, the Jelineks and the Frieds—yes, I know they were arrested with me. But why is Pavel Kropachek here, the art historian who helped Mirek in his work among the intellectuals? Who else but Mirek and I knew about him? And why is that tall young man with the mashed face trying to pretend we don't know each other? I really don't know him. But who can he be? Why, it's Shtych. Shtych? Dr. Zdenek Shtych? Heavens, that means they have broken into the physicians' unit. But who knew about them besides Mirek and me? And why did they ask me about the group of intellectuals in that grilling in the cell? How did they ever come to connect me with the work among the intelligentsia? Who knew anything whatever about that except Mirek and me?

It was not hard to find the answer, but it was a cruel blow —Mirek must have talked, must have given us all away. For a moment I hoped that he hadn't told everything, but they soon brought up another group of prisoners and I saw what he had done.

Everyone who was supposed to be in the National Revolutionary Committee of Czech intellectuals was here: Vladimir Vanchura, the author; Prof. Felber and his son; Bedrich Vaclavek, disguised beyond recognition; Bozhena Pulpanova, Jindrich Elbl, the sculptor Dvorak. Mirek must have told everything about the work among the intelligentsia.

The first period in the Petchek Building had not been exactly easy on me, but this blow was the worst I had to bear. I had expected death, but not betrayal. No matter how lenient I was in judging him, no matter what ameliorating circumstances I thought up for him, in spite of all I hoped

[37]

that Mirek had not told them, I could find no other word for it than betrayal. This was not wavering or weakness, nor even the feverish floundering of a man tortured close to death, which one can forgive. Now I realized how they learned my name that very first night. Now I understood how Anny Jiraskova got in here, for I had met Mirek a couple of times at her house. Now I knew why Kropachek and Dr. Shtych were here.

I was taken to number 400 almost daily after that, and daily discovered new details. It was tragic and fearful. Here was a man with courage; he had not feared bullets when he fought on the Spanish front, had not bowed his head during the cruel life in a concentration camp in France. But now he had gone pale before the switch in the hand of a Gestapo man, and he had betrayed us to save his teeth. How superficial his conviction and his courage when they broke in order to save a few blows. He was strong while in a group, surrounded by comrades with the same ideas. He was strong while he thought of them. But when he was isolated, alone among the probing enemy, he lost his strength completely. He lost everything because he began to think about himself. To save his skin he sacrificed his comrades, gave way to cowardice and betrayed in cowardice.

He forgot that it were better to die than to decipher the material they found in his room. He spelled it all out for them. He gave them names, gave the addresses where they lived secretly. He took a Gestapo agent to an appointment with Shtych. He sent the police to Dvorak's home for a meeting with Vaclavek and Kropachek. He handed over

Anny. He betrayed Lida, a brave girl who loved him. It took only a few blows to make him tell half of all he knew. And when he thought I was dead and there was no one he had to be responsible to, he told all the rest.

He did not hurt me in all that. I was already in the hands of the Gestapo—what could hurt me now? But his answers laid the basis for a whole series of investigations, started a chain of evidence which led back to me. He revealed things which they were extremely glad to know. Did I, and most of any group, live through the period of martial law, just for this? My group couldn't have existed after he and I were gone. But if he had kept his mouth shut, his other group would have lived and gone on working even after he and I were long dead.

A coward loses more than his own life. This one deserted a wonderful army and surrendered to the dirtiest of the enemy. Even though still alive, he is already dead because he excluded himself from his group. He tried later to make amends, but was never accepted back. That ostracism is much worse to bear in prison than anywhere else.

Imprisonment and solitude are two thoughts often confused in people's minds, but that is a great mistake. A prisoner is not alone. A prison is a community, and even the strictest confinement cannot tear one from the group—unless he excludes himself. The brotherhood of the enslaved is subjected to pressure which strengthens, concentrates it, and makes it more sensitive. It penetrates walls, which live, speak and tap out signals. Brotherhood embraces the cells of each corridor, which are related in common duties, common worries, have the same guards and exercise periods together in the fresh air. When they meet outdoors, one word or gesture is sufficient to pass on news or sometimes to save a human life. Brotherhood unites the prisoners who go to hearings, in groups, sit together in the Cinema and return together. It is a brotherhood of very few words and immense services, for the grasp of a hand or the gift of a cigarette can crack the cage you have been placed in and liberate you from the solitude which was intended to break you. Cells have hands; you feel how they hold you from falling when you return tortured from a grilling. They feed you when others are driving you to death by hunger. Cells have eyes which watch you as you leave for the execution, and you know that you must walk erect because you are their brother and must not weaken them with a wavering step. This is a brotherhood bleeding at many wounds, but unconquerable. Without its support you could not bear one-tenth of your fated burden. Neither you nor any man.

If I am able to continue this tale (for we know not the day nor the hour) Number 400 will appear frequently, as it does at the head of this chapter. I thought of it first as a room, and my first meditation there was far from happy. It is not a room, however, but a collective, a purposeful and fighting group, even a happy group.

It started in 1940, as the work of the Gestapo anti-Communist unit increased. It was a branch for Communists of the Domestic Imprisonment Department, a waiting room for Communists in order to avoid their having to be led up from the first floor to the fourth every time the Gestapo officials wished to ask them another question. They thought this made their work easier; that was their idea in opening this branch Cinema.

If you put two prisoners together, however, especially if they are Communists, you have an organization in five minutes, which sets out to upset all your plans. In 1942 the Cinema received the name Communist Central, and went through many changes. Thousands and thousands of comrades, men and women, took their seats in turn on its benches. But one thing never changed—the spirit of a collective, devoted to battle and convinced of final victory.

Number 400 was a very advanced trench on the battlefield, completely surrounded by the enemy, under an avalanche of fire from all sides, but never for a moment dreaming of surrender. The red flag flies high here. The absolute unity of the whole nation fighting for its liberty is expressed in this collective solidarity.

Down in the main Cinema paced guards of the SS in high boots; they shouted at you every time you winked your eyes. Up in Number 400 Czech inspectors and agents from the police department were on duty, men who entered Gestapo service as interpreters, either voluntarily or on orders from their superiors, and did their duty as Gestapo henchmen—or as Czechs. Sometimes a mixture of both. It was not necessary to sit at attention here with your hands on your knees and your eyes staring straight ahead. You could sit easily, look around, move your hands. You could dó even more, depending on which of the three sorts of guards were on duty.

In Number 400 you made profound studies of the human

animal. The nearness of death stripped each of us naked. Even those who wore the red arm-bands as Communists under investigation or suspected of cooperation with the Communists, and those who were set here to guard us and who helped in the investigations in a nearby room. In that other room words were your shield or your weapon during the grilling; here in Number 400 you could not hide behind words. Here they do not weigh your words, but what is in you, what you are made of. By this time there was left in you only what is most important in life. By this time all that tempered, weakened or beautified your fundamental personality had been blasted away by the storms which come before death. Only the subject and predicate remained: the loyal resist, the traitor betrays, the hero struggles, the weakling gives up. In each of us there is strength and weakness, courage and fear, firmness and wavering, purity and dirt. Here only one or the other remains. Yes—or no. If anyone tried to dance adroitly between the two extremes, he was as conspicuous as if he had put a yellow feather in his hat or danced in a funeral procession with cymbals in his hands.

There were men like that, of course, among both the prisoners and the Czech inspectors and agents. During investigations they burned a candle to their god in the Reich, and in Number 400 burned another to the bolshevik devil. In the presence of the German commissar they could knock your teeth out trying to make you confess the name of your courier; in Number 400 they would give you a hunk of bread to ease the hunger. In a search unit they would steal everything of value in your home; in Number 400 they would give you half a cigarette from their booty to show how they sympathized with you. There were others—a slightly different variety from the first—who never hurt you on their own initiative, but still less offered you any help. They always had their own skins in mind, and proved extremely sensitive barometers of the political weather. When they were tense and very officious, you could tell that the Germans were making progress toward Stalingrad. When they were affable enough to start a conversation with a prisoner, you knew that the Germans had been beaten back in Stalingrad. If they begin to tell you about their ancient Czech forebears or that they had been forced into service with Gestapo—excellent: the Red Army is certainly marching on Rostov. Still another sort of creature sticks his hands in his pockets while you are drowning, and lends you a hand after you have pulled yourself out on the bank.

That sort instinctively felt the strength of the collective in Number 400 and tried to draw close to it because of that strength. But they never belonged to it. There was another sort who never even guessed there was such a collective. I would call them the murderers, but murderers are of the human race. They were the Czech-speaking beasts, with sticks and irons in their hands, who tortured us so that many a German commissar fled from the sight. They hadn't even enough hypocrisy to control their passions, for the sake of either their own nation or the Reich. They tortured and murdered for pleasure, knocked out our teeth, burst our eardrums, gouged out our eyes, kicked us in the groin, or beat our brains out for no reason but to satisfy the cruelty within themselves. You saw them every

[43]

day and had to bear their presence, which filled the air with croaking and blood. The only defense you had against them was the firm faith that they would not escape justice in the end, even if they murdered every last witness to their crimes.

At the same table with these types sat men who ought in justice to be written with a capital M—Men. Those who used prison rules to protect the prisoners, who helped build the prison collective in Number 400 and belonged to it with all their hearts and all their courage. Their greatness stands out the more, since they were not Communists; on the contrary, they may have worked against the Communists as agents of the Czech police. But they realized the significance of the Communists for the whole nation when they saw us battle against the invader, and from that moment assisted each of us who held true and loyal even on those prison benches.

Many of our soldiers outside would have wavered had they had any conception of what awaited them once they fell into the hands of the Gestapo. These loyal men inside had the horrors before their eyes every day, every hour. Every hour they lived with the expectation of being set among the prisoners and being tested worse than they. But they didn't waver. They helped save the lives of thousands and tempered the suffering of those whose lives they couldn't save. The name of hero belongs to them. Without them Number 400 could never have become what it was to thousands of Communists: a spot of light in a black building, a trench in the rear of the enemy, the center of the battle for freedom right in the den of the invader.

[44]

Chapter V

CHARACTERS AND PROFILES I

ONE THING I would ask of you who live through this period of history: never forget the people who take part in this struggle. Remember the good and the bad. Collect all the evidence you can on those who fell both for you and for themselves. The present will eventually become past history; it will be called a great epoch with nameless heroes who made history. They all had names, faces, hopes and longings, however, and for that reason the suffering of the least of them is no less than of the first, whose names will be preserved. I only wish you felt close to all of them, as though you knew them, as though they were of your own family, or even were you yourself.

Whole families of heroes have been killed off. Choose some one of them to love as you would your own son or daughter; be as proud of them as of some great man who lived for the future. Each one who truly lived into the future and gave his life to make the future beautiful is of a stature to be carved in stone. And the others, who tried to build out of the dust of the past a dike against the flood of revolution, are puppets of rotting wood, even if their shoulders are gilded with the marks of rank. Even these figures it is necessary to see in the flesh, in their pitiful meanness, their cruelty and ridiculousness, for they also provide material for our conception of the future.

The following evidence of one eye-witness consists only of such sketches as I was able to jot down on one little sector and without much perspective. Mere outlines of personal profiles, of great characters and also of small figures.

THE JELINEKS

Joseph and Marie. He a street-car conductor and she a domestic servant. You should see their apartment. Smooth, simple, modern furniture, a bookcase, a statuette, pictures on the walls—and clean, clean beyond belief. You would say that Marie's whole being is enclosed in that home and that she knows nothing of the rest of the world. But she has worked long in the Communist party, and dreamt her own dreams of social justice. They both worked devotedly, quietly—and never drew back when the invasion made heavy demands on them.

After three years in the underground, the police broke into their home. They stood side by side, their hands raised above their heads—touching.

MAY 19, 1943

Tonight they drag my Gustina off to Poland "for labor." To the galleys, to death from typhus. She has only a few weeks of life left, perhaps two or three months. And my case has been turned over to the court. There will be about four more weeks of examination in Pankrats, and then two or three months to the end. These notes will never be finished. I shall try to write what I can if there is a chance in the next few days. But I can't write today. My mind and heart are full of Gustina, a noble and warm person, a precious devoted friend in a life which has been deep but never exactly peaceful.

Evening after evening I sing her the song she loves best. Of the bluish grass of the steppes, whispering the glorious tales of partisan battles. Of a Cossack girl who fought for freedom by the side of her husband, of her bravery, and how after one battle they couldn't raise her from the ground.

Oh, my courageous comrade, what strength is in that little being and its finely carved face! What tenderness in those great childlike eyes! The endless struggle and frequent absences made us eternal lovers who have a hundred times re-lived the burning moments of the first caress and first union. It is always one pulse which beats in our two hearts, one breath which we two breathe in moments of bliss and hours of anxiety, excitement or grief.

For years we have worked together and helped each other, as only a friend can help a friend. For years she has been my first reader and first critic; it was hard to write when I could not feel her eyes on me. For years we have stood together in the struggles in which our life has been rich. For years we have wandered hand in hand over the land we love. We have had many trials and many great joys, for we have been rich with the wealth of the poor— the wealth which is within us.

Gustina? Look, this is Gustina:

It was during martial law, in the middle of June, a year ago. She saw me for the first time six weeks after our

[47]

arrest, after all those calamitous days when she strove alone in her cell against the various rumors of my death. They called her in to soften me up.

"Persuade him," said the chief of the department as he placed us face to face, "persuade him to be reasonable. If he won't think of himself, make him think of you at least. You have an hour to think it over. If you are still stubborn, you will be shot tonight. Both of you."

She stroked me with her eyes and said simply:

"Mr. Commissar, that is no threat for me. That is my last and greatest wish. If you execute him, execute me too."

That is my Gustina, immense love and great strength.

They can take our lives, can't they, Gustina? But cannot take our love or our honor.

Can you imagine, people, how we shall live if we ever meet after all this is past? To meet again in a life of freedom, beautiful with creative liberty? When we have achieved what we have longed for, and worked so patiently for, and for which now we go to die? Even though dead, we shall still live in a bit of your great happiness because we have invested our lives in it. That gives us joy, even though it is hard to part.

But they did not let us say farewell, embrace, or even grasp hands. Only the prison collective which communicates between Pankrats and Karlovo Square brings us occasional news of each other's fate. You know, Gustina, and I know that we shall probably never see each other again. And yet I hear your voice at a distance calling: Good-bye, my love, till we meet.

Till we meet again, my Gustina!

MY LAST WILL

I had nothing but my library. The Gestapo destroyed that.

I wrote many articles on cultural and political questions, studies and reviews on literature and the drama, much journalistic work. Many of these writings belonged merely to the passing day, and died with the day. Let those lie. Some belong to life. I hoped that Gustina would publish them, but little chance of that now. I therefore ask my comrade Ladya Stoll to select the best of them and group them in five books:

1. Political articles and discussions.
2. Selected reports on domestic affairs.
3. Notes from the Soviet Union.
4. and 5. Literary and dramatic studies and articles.

Most of them will be found in *Tvorba* (*Creative Art*), *Rude Pravo* (*Red Rights*), others in *Kmen, Pramen, Proletkult, Doba, The Socialist, Avantgard* and other literary and political periodicals.

My study on Julius Zeyer is in the hands of Girgal, a publisher whom I love for the courage with which he published my *Bozhena Nemcova* during the occupation. Part of the study on Sabin and notes on Jan Neruda are secreted somewhere in the building where lived the Jelineks, Vysushils and Suchaneks, most of them now dead.

I began a novel about our generation. Two chapters are with my parents, the rest has probably been destroyed. Manuscripts of several tales I saw among the papers in my Gestapo file.

I bequeath my love for Jan Neruda to some historian

[49]

of literature yet to be born. He was our greatest poet; he saw far beyond us into the future. There is no study of him yet which fully understands and appreciates him. The picture of Neruda as a proletarian has not been drawn. He was born on the edge of Smichov, a workingman's section, and the material for "Cemetery Flowers" he gathered around the Ringhoffer Mills. Without that background you cannot understand Neruda from his "Cemetery Flowers" to the piece called "May 1st, 1890." The majority — even so clear-thinking a critic as Shalda — suppose that Neruda's journalistic work interfered with his poetry. That is nonsense. It was just because Neruda was a journalist that he was able to create such magnificent works as the *Ballads, Sonnets, Hymns for Friday Devotions* and most of his *Simple Motifs.* Journalism is exhausting and distracting, but it brings one into direct contact with the reader and teaches one to create even poetry—if one is as honest a journalist as Neruda. Without the newspaper, Jan Neruda might have written many volumes of poetry, but none could have lived for centuries, as his present works live. Someone may yet complete *Sabina.* It is worth the effort.

Because of their love and simple sublimity I wished to insure my parents a sunny autumn for their lives. That purpose gave meaning to much of my work. I only hope my going will not cloud their days. "The worker is mortal, but the work lives" and I shall be constantly with them in the very warmth and light which surrounds them.

I ask my sisters, Liba and Vera, with song and laughter to help Dad and Mamma forget the gap which has been left in our family. They shed many tears when they came to visit us in the Petchek Building, but joy lives in them and that is why we love each other so. They strew joy all about them—let nothing ever steal their happiness.

I press the hand of every comrade who lives through this last battle, and those who come after us. A handclasp for Gustina and for me; we who did our duty.

And I repeat, we live for happiness, for that we went to battle, for that we die. Let grief never be connected with our name.

May 19, 1943

J. F.

MAY 22, 1943

Signed and sealed. The investigating judge finished with me yesterday. The case moves even faster than I foresaw. It looks as though they were in somewhat of a hurry. My co-defendants are Lida Placha and Mirek. His defection did not gain him much.

Everything was cold and correct before the investigating judge, cold enough to make us shiver. But at Gestapo headquarters things were pretty lively, frightening, but still a part of life. There was passion there, the passion of fighters on one side and of hunters on the other, of beasts of prey or ordinary robbers. Several on that other side have convictions of a sort. Before the investigator, however, there was nothing but an official act. The big lug with the hooked cross on his lapels indicated a conviction which did not exist inside him. They were the shield behind which hid a pitiful little official, trying merely to live

[51]

through this era somehow. He is neither good nor bad to the defendants. He neither smiles nor scowls. He only performs an official function. Instead of blood he has very thin soup in his veins.

They copied out evidence, quoted paragraphs of the law, and signed. There are about six charges of treason there, intrigues against the Reich, preparations for armed uprising, and I don't know what all. Any one of them would be sufficient.

For thirteen months now I have been fighting here for my life and that of others, with ruses and with spirit. Their party platform talks about Nordic strategems, but I think I trumped them at that. I have lost out simply because they hold the ax, in addition to their trickery.

That duel is thus at an end. Now begins the waiting. Two or three weeks until the indictment is worked out, then the journey to the Reich, waiting for the trial, the sentence, and finally the hundred days of waiting for execution. That is my outlook—a future of four or perhaps five months. A lot can happen in that time. Everything could be changed in that time. Perhaps. There is no way I can guess from here. A rapid change of events outside could, however, also hasten our finish. So even that might not be helpful.

This is a race between the war and hope. A race of one sort of death against another sort of death. Which will come first — the death of fascism or my death? Is that merely my private question? Oh, no, it is asked by tens of thousands of prisoners, by millions of soldiers. It is also asked by tens of millions of people in all Europe and around the world. Some have more hope; some less. But that is really only illusory. The horrors with which the decay of capitalism has engulfed the world threaten everybody to the utter limit. Hundreds of thousands of people shall die—and what fine people—before those who remain are able to say: I outlived fascism.

It is a matter of months, and soon it will be a matter of days. But those will be the cruelest days. I have often imagined how tragic it would be to be the last soldier to be shot through the heart by the last bullet in the last second of a war. But someone must be that last soldier to fall. If I knew that I could be that last man to fall, I would go this moment.

The short time left me in Pankrats does not permit me to give these notes the form I would wish. I must be briefer. Give more attention to people and less to the period of history. They are most important.

I began to describe the Jelinek couple, simple people in whom you would not have seen heroes in normal times. At the time of their arrest, they stood next each other, their hands above their heads—he pale, she with that tubercular flush below her temples. Her eyes showed some fright when she saw how the Gestapo wrecked her model apartment in five minutes. Then she turned her head slowly toward her husband and asked:

"What happens now, Joe?"

He never had much to say, had to search for his words; and talking excited him. Now he replied calmly, without effort or pathos:

[53]

"We shall go off to die, Marie."

She did not scream or even shudder. With a graceful movement, she lowered her right hand and grasped his, there before the mouths of the pistols. That earned both of them the first blow in the face. She wiped her cheek, looked the invaders up and down, and said almost comically:

"Such handsome young fellows," she said, raising her voice, "such handsome fellows and such brutes."

She took their measure correctly. A few hours later they carried her out of the office of the "examining commissar" beaten almost to unconsciousness, but they could not beat anything out of her. Neither then nor later did she ever give anything away.

I cannot say just what happened to them during the time that I lay in my cell unfit for a hearing, but I do know that they told nothing in all that time. They were waiting for me to give the word. How often he was bound wrists to ankles and beaten endlessly. But never talked until I was there and could give him a sign with my eyes what he should admit so that we could get on with the examination.

His wife was sensitive and compassionate, as I knew her before the arrest. In the whole period at Gestapo, however, I did not see a tear in her eyes. Her home was her pride, but when the comrades outside wished to comfort her by sending in word that they knew who had stolen her furniture and were keeping constant watch on him, she replied:

"The devil with the furniture. Don't waste time worrying

about that. There are much more important things to do, and right now they have to work double to take our places. First we have to scrub out this place, and if I live through that, I'll be able to take care of my house myself."

One day they took the Jelineks away, each to a different place. I searched in vain for any trace of their fate, for people have a way of disappearing utterly after Gestapo handling—scattered in a thousand cemeteries. Oh, what a crop will rise one day from that frightful seeding.

Her last message was:

"Chief, tell them outside not to grieve for me, and for no one to be intimidated by my fate. I did my duty as a worker, and shall die the same way, too."

She was only "a domestic." Never had much education, and did not know that brave message centuries ago:

Pilgrim, tell the Lacedaemonians that we lie dead, as the law required.

THE VYSUSHILS

Lived in the same building, right next the Jelineks. They were also named Joseph and Marie. A minor official's family, a little older than their neighbors. He was seventeen when they drafted him and sent him into the First World War, a tall youth from Nusle. A few weeks later they brought him back with a smashed knee, which never healed properly. They first met in a hospital in Brno, where she was a nurse. She was eight years older than he, having left an unhappy marriage—and possibly this tall

[55]

railway clerk and the lady got entangled in something normally forbidden.

He was arrested shortly after me, and I was horrified the first time I saw him here. How much would be lost if he talked! But he didn't. He was brought here because of a few political leaflets which he gave a pal to read—but he never got further than leaflets.

Some time ago an indiscretion of Pokorny and Pixova gave away the fact that Honza Cherny lived in the apartment of Mrs. Vysushilova's sister. Thus they "examined" Joe Vysushil two days after my arrest, tried to beat out of him something about the last Mohican of our Central Committee. The third day he came into number 400 and sat down very carefully—it hurts like the devil to sit on open wounds. I glanced at him with both anxiety and encouragement. He replied in the forthright Nusle manner:

"When I refuse, they get nothing for all their work on my backside."

I knew that couple well—how much they loved each other and how lonesome they were whenever they were separated for a day or two. Months passed now. How sad the wife must be in that attractive home above Michle, alone at the age when solitude is three times worse than death. How many plots she must have invented to bring her husband back to the little idyl in which they comically called each other Mummykins and Daddykins. But she found only one way to get along—to keep at the underground job, to do the work of two.

Thus she sat alone at the table on New Year's Eve, 1943, with his picture where he used to sit. As it struck midnight, she clicked her glass with his at that empty place and drank to his health and his quick return—chiefly that he should live till liberty.

A month later she was arrested also. Many of us in number 400 shuddered because she was one of the people outside through whom we kept contact open.

She didn't drop a word.

They did not beat her; she was so ill that she would have died under their blows. They tortured her worse—with imagination.

A few days before her arrest they took her husband off for labor in Poland. Now they told her:

"Look, what a hard life that is, even for a healthy man. But your husband is a cripple and will never stand it. He will drop dead there, and you will never see him again. Then where will you look for a husband—at your age? So, be reasonable and tell us what you know, and we shall return him to you right away."

He will die somewhere there, my Joe, poor Joe! Who knows what sort of a death? They have killed my sister, they will kill my husband and I shall be left alone, all alone till death. Whom could I find at this age? But I could save him. They would bring him back—for a price. No, it won't be I who will pay that price, and it would not be he if I got him back that way.

She never dropped a word.

She disappeared in one of the nameless transports of Gestapo. And soon after came word that her Joe died in Poland.

LIDA

The first time I went to the Baxas' was in the evening. Only Josey was home and a tiny creature with lively eyes whom they called Lida. She was hardly more than a child, staring curiously at my whiskers and happy that some new and interesting thing had come in to keep her amused for a while.

We became friends quickly. It turned out, to my surprise, that this child was almost nineteen, Josey's half-sister. Her family name is Placha (which means timid) but she does not have that characteristic herself. She is fond of amateur dramatics.

I became her confidant, which made me realize that I am an elderly gentleman in spite of everything. She confessed all her youthful sorrows and youthful dreams to me, and ran to me to decide her arguments with her sister or brother-in-law. She was quick-tempered as young girls are, and spoiled as late children are.

She went with me the first time I left the house after living there half a year. An elderly man with a limp was less noticeable if he walked out with his daughter than if he were alone. Those we passed looked at her rather than at me. That is why she went with me on my walks, that is why she went with me to my first illegal meeting. That is why she moved into my first secret apartment. Thus—as the indictment now says—thus it developed naturally that she became my underground courier.

She does it happily, without worrying too much about what the work is or what it means. It was something new and interesting, something which not everybody does, and has a taste of adventure. That is all she needed.

As long as she worked on small matters, I didn't wish to tell her much about it. The less she knew if she were caught, the better she could defend herself—better than if she had a feeling of guilt.

Lida developed fast, and could take much more responsibility than running to the Jelineks with some small message. It was time to tell her what it was all about, and I began to teach her. It was a regular school, and Lida learned greedily and happily. To all appearances, she was the same happy girl, light-hearted and a little flippant, but inside she was quite changed. She grew and began to think deeply.

In this work she became acquainted with Mirek. He had already done a lot of work and was able to tell about it convincingly. He made quite an impression on her. She perhaps missed judgment on his basic traits, but in that I misjudged him also. The important thing was that his work and his evident conviction brought him closer to her than other youths.

Love grew fast in her and set deep roots.

Early in 1942 she began hesitatingly to ask questions about membership in the party. I had never before seen her so hesitant; she had never taken anything so seriously. I weighed the matter, continued with her instruction. I still wished to test her.

In February, 1942, she was voted into the party directly by the Central Committee. We walked home through a heavy frosty night; she was silent, though usually quite talkative. Crossing a field near the house, she suddenly stopped and in the silence in which you could hear the snow crystals settling, said ever so quietly:

"I know that this is the most important day of my life, for I no longer belong to myself. I promise you that I will never disappoint you no matter what happens."

A great deal happened after that, and she never failed us.

She maintained our most confidential relations with the higher leadership. She had the most delicate and most dangerous jobs of making contact with groups which had been cut off, and of warning workers who were threatened with acute danger. When things went wrong for the higher command or our secret hideout was in danger, Lida slipped through like an eel and set things right. She did the important things just as she had done the small, as a matter of course, with happy light-heartedness, beneath which was now a firm sense of responsibility.

She was arrested a month after us. Mirek mentioned her when he talked, and then they found out that she had helped her sister and brother-in-law to escape into the underground. She tossed her head and played the temperamental role of a light-hearted girl who doesn't suspect that she has done anything illegal, which can have dire consequences for her.

She knew a great deal, but didn't tell a thing. And most important: she kept right on working. Her surroundings and methods changed, her tasks were different, but she did not drop her hands in her lap in any sense of the word. Her duty to the party had not changed. She did what she was given to do fast, exactly and devotedly. If it was necessary somehow to straighten out a complicated situation in order to save someone outside, Lida took it on with an innocent face. She became a trusty in the women's section of Pankrats and scores of unknown people outside were saved from arrest by messages which she got through. After almost a year of this, one of her messages was caught and put an end to this "career" for her.

Now she is going with us to trial in the Reich. She is the only one of our group who has any reasonable hope of living till liberty. She is young. If we should not be here, please don't lose her. She needs to learn a lot. Teach her and don't let her be stunted, but don't let her become proud of herself or content with what she has accomplished. She has stood the test of the toughest struggles. She has passed through fire and has proved to be of excellent mettle.

MY COMMISSAR

He does not belong among the characters, but he is an interesting figure—noticeably grander than the rest.

Ten years ago in Flora Cafe, in Vinohrady, when you wished to tap your money on the table or were about to call out, "the check, head waiter," a tall thin man suddenly appeared beside you in black tails. He had swum quickly between the chairs, without a sound, like a water-spider, and laid your check before you. He had the rapid, silent movements of a beast of prey, and eyes which take in everything at once. You did not even have to state your

[61]

order. He would tell the waiter: "White coffee without whipped cream for the third table" or "Pastry and the *People's Paper* for the left window table." He was an excellent head waiter for the customers, and a good colleague for the other employees.

I did not know him then, however. I got acquainted with him much later, at the Jelineks, when he held a pistol in his hand instead of a pencil, and was pointing it at me: "That one interests me most."

To tell the truth, we both interested each other from then on.

He had inherent intelligence, and a great advantage over the others in that he understood people. He would have been a big success in the criminal police for that reason. Little criminals and murderers, the declassé and the isolated would not have hesitated to open their hearts to him, since they worry only about saving their skins. But not many of these self-savers fall into the hands of the political police. Here they cannot measure police wits merely against the wits of a man they have caught, but against a power much greater. Here they are pitted against convictions, the wisdom of a group to which their victim belongs. Trickery and blows cannot break convictions.

You will not find any strong internal conviction in "my commissar." If there is in some of those others, it is combined with stupidity—not with cunning, not with knowledge of people or any ideals. If they have been successful on the whole, it is because the struggle has lasted too long and in too restricted a space, under conditions incomparably more difficult than any previous underground struggle.

The Russian Bolsheviks used to say that a really good underground worker can last two years, but if things got too hot for them in Moscow they could disappear to Petrograd and from Petrograd to Odessa, lose themselves among the millions of city inhabitants where no one knew them. Here we have only Prague, Prague, Prague, where half the people know you and where most of the enemy agents are concentrated. In spite of that, we have held out for years and there are comrades who have worked underground for five years without Gestapo discovering them. That is because we have learned many things. Yes, but it is also because the enemy, though strong and cruel, has not learned much more than to destroy.

There are three men in Section 11-A who have the reputation of being the severest eradicators of communism and have won the black-white-red ribbon for courage in the war against the internal enemy—Friedrich, Zander and "my commissar," Joseph Böhm. They have very little to say about Hitler's National Socialism, for they know very little about it. They are not in the fight for a political idea, but merely for themselves. Each in his own way.

Zander—a trifling little person with exaggerated gall—knows more than the rest about police methods, but still more about financial transactions. He was transferred for a few months from Prague to Berlin, but soon succeeded in being sent back. Service in the capital of the Reich was a demotion for him—and a financial sacrifice. A colonial official in dark Africa or in Prague is a more powerful master than in Berlin, and has much better opportunity to increase his bank account. Zander is very industrious, likes to investigate and question while at dinner to show how hard he works. He needs to prove official diligence so that people will not notice that he has still greater unofficial interests. Pity on anyone who falls into his hands, but double pity on whoever has a bank-book at home or any securities. That man will die in short order, for bank-books and securities are Zander's passion. He is considered the ablest of all German officials—in that direction. In that he is slightly different from his Czech assistant—Smola—who is a gentleman robber, and does not take your life if he gets your money.

Friedrich is the tall, thin, sallow type with evil eyes and an evil smile. He came to Czechoslovakia as a Gestapo spy in 1937, for the purpose of catching and dispatching German Communists who took refuge in the Republic. His passion is corpses. He does not admit anyone's innocence; whoever crosses the threshold of his office is guilty. He likes to tell women that their husbands have died in concentration camp or have been executed. He likes to pull seven urns of ashes out of the desk drawer and show them to whomever he is examining:

"I beat those seven to death with my own hands, and you shall be the eighth."

Now he has eight urns in his desk, for he beat Jan Zhizhka to death.

He likes to finger through files of papers on his various cases and repeat:

"Settled. Closed case!"

But he likes to torture women most of all.

His love of luxury is an asset in his police activities. A

nicely furnished home or a successful business is certain to hasten your death, that is all.

His Czech assistant—Nerger—is half a head shorter as to height. But that is the only difference between them.

My commissar, Böhm, has no passion for money or for corpses, although there are not many less on his list than on those of the first two. He is an adventurer with a longing to be somebody. He is also an old Gestapo man. He worked in the Napoleon Room when Hitler met Beran alone in the most confidential conferences. Böhm added whatever Beran did not tell Hitler himself. But that was nothing compared to the opportunity to hunt people down, to become lord of their lives and their deaths, to order the death of whole families!

It did not always have to turn out quite so tragically to keep him satisfied. But he felt the need to excel; that could be even worse than murdering whole families.

He built up the greatest network of agents-provocateur. He became the hunter with the largest band of dogs, and he hunted. He often hunted merely for the pleasure of the hunt. Examinations were for him a dreary business; his chief interest was arresting and then seeing people stand before him waiting for his decision. Once he arrested two hundred Prague street-car conductors and motormen with some city bus-drivers, whom he herded down the center of the street, stopping all traffic and causing panic in the transportation system. Was he happy! Then he let a hundred fifty of them go, satisfied that a hundred and fifty families would talk about him as a kind man.

His usual cases were unimportant, but complicated and

ramifying. I was an exception for he caught me by accident.

"You are my biggest case," he would tell me often and sincerely. He was proud that one of his cases was among the most important of them all. That may even have extended my life a little.

We lied to each other with all our strength and constantly, but with a distinction. The difference was that I always knew when he lied, he often did not know it. When a lie was exposed, however, we passed over it with a tacit understanding not to mention it again. I have a feeling that he was not so anxious to discover the truth as merely to preserve his biggest case unblemished.

Sticks and steel were not the only tools he used in examinations. He preferred to persuade than to threaten, according to his estimate of his man. He did not torture me once, except perhaps that first night. But when he needed to, he loaned me to someone else for that.

He was certainly more interesting and complex than all the others. He had a richer imagination and knew how to use it. We often rode out to an imaginary conference in Branik, where we sat in a beer garden and watched the people streaming by.

Meditating over them, he would say:

"We arrested you, and see, nothing has changed for them. They walk around just as they used to; they smile or worry about their troubles, just as they used to. The world moves on as though you had never existed. There certainly are some of your former readers among them— do you think any of them has one wrinkle more because of you?"

Sometimes after an all-day examination, he put me in an auto and took me up to the Castle through Neruda Street:

"I know that you love Prague. Look! Don't you ever want to return to it? How beautiful Prague is—and she will be beautiful even after you are gone."

He played the role of the Tempter well. The late summer evening breathed a hint of fall over Prague. It was bluish and misting like the ripening vine, intoxicating like the grape. I longed to gaze till the end of the world . . . but I interrupted him:

". . . and Prague will be much more beautiful after *you* are gone."

He laughed briefly, not meanly, but sadly, and said: "You are a cynic."

He often returned to the talk of that evening:

"When we are no longer here. . . . Then you still do not believe in our victory?"

He asked because he was not sure himself. And listened most attentively as I described the strength and invincibility of the Soviet Union. That was one of my last "examinations."

INTERLUDE OF THE SUSPENDERS

There were suspenders hanging beside the door of the opposite cell. Just ordinary men's suspenders. An article which I have never been fond of. But now we gaze at them with pleasure whenever the door of our cell opens—for in them I see a bit of hope.

When they arrest you, they may beat you within an

inch of your life, or even to death, but they always first take away your necktie, belt or suspenders to prevent your hanging yourself (although it is just as nice to hang yourself with your towel). These dangerous instruments of death are then kept in the prison office until some little Gestapo court decides that you are to be sent somewhere else, to labor, to a concentration camp or to execution. They call you in, return the articles to you with official ceremony—but you may not take them into the cell with you. You have to hang them beside the cell door or over the balustrade opposite, and they hang there until your transport leaves, as visible evidence that one of the occupants of that cell is preparing for involuntary travel.

The suspenders opposite appeared there on the day when I learned about the fate awaiting Gustina. My friend opposite is also being sent for labor, in the same transport as she. The group has not yet left, was suddenly postponed because, they say, the place where they were going for that labor was knocked out by bombs. (This is another pleasant prospect.) No one knows when they will leave now—this evening, perhaps tomorrow, or perhaps a week or two weeks later. The suspenders still hang opposite, and I know that as long as I can see them there, Gustina is still here in Prague. So I watch them with pleasure and love, as though they were someone who is helping her. They win her a day, two, three days' respite . . . who knows what those few days may mean? Perhaps one of them will bring her salvation.

That is the way we all live here. Last year, last month, today, tomorrow—our eyes are constantly turned to the

[68]

morrow in which lies hope. Your fate may be sealed, you are to be shot day after tomorrow—but, oh, the many things that can happen in that tomorrow! Just live till tomorrow, and that may change everything. Things are so extremely unstable, who knows what can happen tomorrow? The tomorrows pass; thousands fall and there is no tomorrow for them. But the live continue living in unflagging hope—who knows what can happen tomorrow?

The silliest rumors rise from this state of mind. Every week there is some rosy story about the end of the war, which everyone repeats with a smile stretching from ear to ear. Every week Pankrats whispers some new happy sensation, which we readily believe. You struggle against believing things like that; you suppress false hopes because they do not strengthen the character, but weaken one in the end. Optimism cannot and must not be fed on lies, but only on truth which sees clearly the end of the war in the only way that it can possibly end. The fundamental faith in truth is within oneself. And the faith that one day will be decisive, that a day gained may be the one which will lift you across the boundary between the life which you hate to give up and the death which threatens.

There are not so very many days in a human life. And yet you want them to pass fast, faster, as fast as ever possible. Fleeting time, intractable time, which usually bleeds one's life away, is here one's greatest friend. How strange!

Tomorrow has become yesterday. Day after tomorrow is today—and then is gone. The suspenders still hang by the door of the cell opposite.

[69]

Chapter VI

MARTIAL LAW 1942

May 27th, 1943.

It was just a year ago.

They led me from another grilling down to the Cinema. That was our daily route: from Number 400 down stairs for the dinner which they brought from Pankrats, then back up to the fourth floor. But that day they did not take us back up after noon.

You sit and eat. The benches full of prisoners, busy with their spoons and chewing. It looks almost human. If all of us who will be dead tomorrow should of a sudden turn into skeletons, the ring of spoons on our earthenware bowls would change into the grating of bones and clopping of jaws. Only nobody thought of that, and no one suspected. Each of us was stoking his body in order to live another week, a month or years.

One could almost say: Good weather. Then suddenly a strange wind struck us, and it was oppressively quiet. Only by the faces of the guards could you guess that something unusual was going on. The proof was that they called us out and lined us up and took us off to Pankrats. Back to Pankrats at noon! That has never happend before. Half a day without any grilling; we are all worn out with questions for which we find no answers. It sounds like a gift from God. But it is not.

In the corridor we meet General Eliash (former Prime Minister under the Protectorate, later executed). Excitement in his eyes, he catches sight of me through the hedge of guards, moves over and whispers:

"It's martial law."

He had no chance to reply to my mute question. Prisoners have only split seconds for the most important communications.

The guards at Pankrats were very much surprised at our early return from Petchek's. The one who led me to my cell gave me enough confidence to tell him what I had heard. I don't know who he is, but he merely shook his head. He knew nothing about martial law—or perhaps he didn't hear my question. Yet, perhaps—and that quiets my anxiety at having asked.

That evening, however, he came and looked into the cell:

"You were right. There has been an attempt to assassinate Heydrich. He is badly wounded. Martial law in Prague."

The next day they line us up down in the corridor to take us for another grilling. Among us is Comrade Victor Synek, the last living member of the Central Committee of the party, who was arrested in February, 1941. A long slim turnkey in an SS uniform waves a piece of white paper before his eyes, on which you can see in bold print:

"*Entlassunge befehl.*" "Discharge Order."

He is laughing crudely:

"So you see, you Jew, you did live through it. Your discharge order! Figs. . . ." At that he draws his finger

[71]

around his neck in the sign that Victor's head will fly off. Otto Synek was the first to be executed under martial law in 1941. His brother Victor is the first victim of martial law in 1942. They take him to Mauthausen for the bump-off, as their elegant expression is.

The route from Pankrats to Petchek building and back now becomes the daily calvary for thousands of prisoners. The SS guards in busses "take revenge for Heydrich." Before they have gone half a mile, blood flows from the faces and mouths of dozens of prisoners beaten with pistol butts. Those who happen to ride with me usually have it easier because my beard is the object of a great many practical jokes, and there is less time for beating the rest of the passengers. As the car jerks along, the guards like to hang onto my whiskers as to a strap in a car, one of their favorite pastimes. That is good preparation for my grillings, which change routine according to the political situation, but invariably end with:

"If you don't come to your senses by tomorrow, you will be shot."

There is nothing very terrifying in that any more. Evening after evening you hear them calling out names down in the corridor. Fifty, a hundred, two hundred people will in a moment be bound hand and foot, laid in autos and carted like slaughter-house cattle to mass execution at Kobylisy. What is the charge against them? First of all that nothing has been proved against them. They were arrested, no connection has been found with any of the major cases, they are unnecessary for further investigation, so they can be used for executions. A satirical lyric which one comrade read to nine others caused the arrest of all of them two months before the assassination. Now they are in death-cells—"for approving the assassination." A woman was arrested six months ago on suspicion that she was circulating underground leaflets. She has never admitted it, nor have they any proof. Nevertheless they have arrested her brothers and sisters, her brothers' wives and sisters' husbands, and are going to murder them all because wiping out whole families of "suspicious persons" is the motto of this martial law. A post-office messenger, who had been arrested by mistake, is standing down in the corridor waiting to be set free. He hears his name called, and they hustle him into the line of those condemned to death, cart him off and shoot him. Only the next day they discover that it was a mistake; someone else with the same name was to have been shot. So they execute the other man, too, and everything is set right. Who can take time to make sure that the people they execute are the right ones? And what is the use, anyway, when their purpose is to kill off the whole nation?

That night I come back very late from my "hearing." Down by the wall stands Vladimir Vanchura with a little bundle of his things at his feet (one of the most talented Czech novelists). I know very well what that means, and he knows also. We grip hands for a moment. I can still see him from the upper corridor, standing with his head slightly bowed and his eyes gazing far, far across our lives. A half hour later they called out his name. . . .

A few days later Milosh Krasny stands facing that same wall, a brave soldier of the revolution, who was arrested in October last year. Unbroken by torture or by solitary confinement. Half turned away from the wall, he is calmly explaining something to the guard standing behind him.

He sees me suddenly, smiles, throws up his head in farewell and goes on talking to the guard:

"This will not help you at all. A lot more of us are going to fall, but you will be defeated in the end. . . ."

Then again one noon, we are standing downstairs in the Petchek building waiting for dinner. They bring in Eliash, with a newspaper under his arm. He points at it and smiles, for he had just read that they proved he had some connection with the assassination (although he had been in prison for the past eight months).

"Bunk!" he said and started on his food.

While returning with the rest of us to Pankrats that evening, he talks about it jokingly. But an hour later they take him from his cell and cart him off to Kobylisy.

The corpses are piling up. They no longer count them in tens, nor in hundreds, but in thousands. The smell of fresh blood tingles in the nostrils of the beasts. They "work" late into the night and on Sundays. They all wear SS uniforms now; this is their celebration, their festival of slaughter. They send to death workers, teachers, farmers, writers, officials; they slaughter men, women and children; murder whole families, exterminate and burn whole villages. Death by lead stalks the land like the plague, and makes no distinction among its victims.

But even in this horror, people still live.

It is unbelievable, but people still live, eat, sleep, make love, work and think about a thousand things which have no connection with death. Back in their minds there is a terrific tension, but they bear it. They do not bow their heads nor fall beneath it.

In the middle of martial law, my commissar took me out

to Branik. The beautiful June was heavy with the sweet of the lindens and late acacia blossoms. A Sunday evening, and the street out to the end of the car-line was not wide enough to hold the stream of returning excursionists. They were cheerful and noisy, delightfully tired, having spent the day in the embrace of the sun and water and of the arms of their lovers. Only death was not visible on their faces, though it walked among them and occasionally aimed his bolt at one of their number. They flop and tumble like rabbits, and are just as cute. Like rabbits! Reach in among them and grab one for your dinner. They huddle together in a corner for a moment, but are soon swarming about again, with their pleasures and worries, full of the joy of life.

I was suddenly transplanted from the walled-up life of prison into this bursting stream of humanity, and the first taste of its sweet bliss was bitter to me.

It should not have been, however.

What I see here is life, and what I have just come from is life. No matter what terrific pressure is applied, life is indestructible. It may be beaten out at one point but bursts forth at a hundred others. It is life, and remains stronger than death. Should that be bitter?

And are we who live in cells, right in the midst of horror, of any different metal than the rest of the nation?

Occasionally I went to my hearings in a police car, in which the guard was quite well-behaved. I could look out the window at the street, at the show-windows, at a flower-stand, at crowds of passers-by, at women. I once told myself that whenever I was able to count nine pairs of pretty legs I wouldn't be executed that day. Then I began to look

[75]

them over, to compare their lines carefully, selected and rejected with excited interest in legs—quite regardless that my life depended upon it, as though just lines and not a life were involved.

They usually brought me back to the cell quite late. Dad Peshek always worried whether I would return at all. He embraced me and I told him whatever news I had heard, who fell at Kobylisy last night. Then we were driven by hunger to eat the disgusting mash of dehydrated vegetables. We sang a cheerful song or, if angry and depressed, played a game of dice which diverted our attention completely for a while. That was the way we spent the evening hours when the door of our cell might open at any moment and the death order sound for one of us.

"You, or you, get downstairs. Take everything with you! Quick!"

But neither of us was called in that period. We lived through that time of horror. We think of it now with surprise at our own feelings. How strangely people are built— we can bear the unbearable.

It is impossible, however, to prevent such times from leaving deep traces on our lives. They lie in little rolls of film under the membrane of our brain, and unroll in the form of insanity some time later in real life—if we ever live that long. Or perhaps they will unfold later in the form of great cemeteries, or green gardens planted with the most precious seed of human lives.

The most precious seed, which will germinate and spring to life one day.

Chapter VII

CHARACTERS AND PROFILES II

PANKRATS

PRISON has two lives. One is locked in the cells, sternly isolated from all the world—and yet related to the world in the closest bonds in the case of political prisoners. The other life is in the long corridors before the cells, a uniformed life in the oppressive half-dusk—a life more isolated than that in the cells, in spite of the figures and little fellows who fill it. That is the life I wish now to describe.

It has fauna of its own, and its own history. If it had not, I could not have made any study of it. I would have known only the front of the stage-setting turned toward us, only its superficially hard and unyielding surface which pressed like a constant weight upon the occupants of the cells. That is how it seemed a year ago, even half a year ago. But now I can see that the surface is full of cracks large enough for faces to look through—poor inquisitive faces, or worried funny faces. All kinds of faces, but each belongs to some human being. The strain of the regime presses on each member of that dim world like a vise, which brings to light whatever he has of human feelings. That is often extremely little; some have perceptibly more humanity than others. The amount forms distinctions and creates types among them. You even find a few whole people here, of course. But these did not require the stress of this regime in order to be helpful to others.

Prison is not a happy institution, but the world in front of the cells is gloomier than that in the cells. Friendship dwells in the cells—and what friendship! The kind which one meets at the front during long-sustained danger, when your life may be in my hands today, and mine in yours tomorrow. There is extremely little friendship among the guards of this regime, however. There cannot be. They are surrounded with the atmosphere of petty spying, they squeal on each other, and always have to be on guard with those whom they officially call "comrades." The best of them, who cannot live without companionship, find it in the cells.

For a long while we did not know each others' names. That didn't matter, for we thought up nicknames for them among ourselves. Some names we gave them, others had been invented by our predecessors and were inherited with the cell. Some of them were called by a different nickname in each cell—that was the mediocre type, neither fish nor fowl, who gave a little extra in one cell but struck them in the face in the next. Such are the seconds of contact with the prisoners which make a permanent impression on the inmates of a cell, one-sided impressions which give rise to nicknames. Sometimes all the cells invent the same nicknames, however, in the case of guards with more marked and consistent characteristics, either good or bad.

Let us take a look at these characters. Take a look at

these little figures! They are not an accidental collection; they are part of the political army of Nazism. They have been carefully selected, the pillars of the regime, the supports on which their society rests——

"THE FIRST-AID MAN"

The tall, fat SS reservist with the weak tenor voice is Rheuss, a school janitor from Cologne on the Rhine. Like all German school janitors, he had taken a course in first-aid and often substituted for the prison medic. He was the first man I had contact with in this place. He dragged me into the cell, laid me out on the bunk, took care of my wounds, laid on my first compresses. Perhaps he really helped to save my life. What was that an expression of? His humanity, or his first-aid course? I don't know. But it was certainly an expression of Nazism when he knocked the teeth out of arrested Jews, or gave them the heaping spoonful of salts or sand which was their universal medicine for all ailments.

"SMARTY"

The talkative, kindhearted Fabian was a driver from the brewery in Czeska Budejovitze. He entered the cell with a broad smile when he brought our food, and never made trouble for us. You would never believe that he could stand outside the cell door for hours listening for some silly little thing with which he could run to his superiors.

"KOKLAR"

Was also a workman from the brewery in Budejovitze.

[79]

There are plenty of them here, German workers from the Sudeten region. Marx once wrote: "It is not important what the worker as an individual thinks or does, but what labor as a class must do to fulfill its historic task." The ones we see here know absolutely nothing about the task of their class. Torn out of their class and placed in opposition to it, they hang in the air ideologically—and will probably in the end hang physically, too.

He joined the Nazis in order to earn an easy living. It turns out to be more complicated than he imagined, however. He has lost his smile since then. He bet on a Nazi victory, but it appears that he bet on a dead horse. He has lost his nerve. As he paced the corridors at night in noiseless slippers, he unconsciously left traces of his dreary thoughts in the dust of the lamp shades.

"Everything stinks," he wrote poetically on one of them, and thought of suicide.

During the day he drives both prisoners and guards with shouts in a hasty, wheezy voice—just to keep up his courage.

ROSSLER

Tall and thin, with a coarse bass voice, Rössler is one of the few here who are able to laugh sincerely. A textile worker from Jablonetz who comes into the cell and discusses for hours.

"How did I get into this? For ten years I hadn't had any regular work, and you know what kind of a life you can have on twenty crowns a week for a whole family.

Then they come along and say: We'll give you work, come along with us. I go and they give me work, me and all the others, we can eat at least, and can have a home. We can live again. Socialism? Well, it isn't much good. I imagined it differently but it is better than what we had before.

"It isn't? The war? Oh, I didn't want war. I didn't want other people to die; I only wanted to live myself.

"What? That I am helping the war whether I wish to or not? What shall I do? Have I hurt anyone here? If I go, others will come in my place, perhaps worse people. Would that help anybody? After the war I'll go back to the factory. . . .

"Who do you think is going to win? Not us? You? Then what will become of us?

"The end of us? That's too bad. I imagined it differently."

And he leaves the cell with long listless strides.

Half an hour later he comes back with a question on what it is really like in the Soviet Union.

"IT"

One morning we were waiting down in the main corridor of Pankrats for them to take us off to hearings in Petchek Building. We had to stand here every day with our foreheads close against the wall so that none could see what went on behind us. That morning I heard a new voice:

"I don't want to see anything. I don't want to hear anything! You don't know me, but you will get acquainted with me!"

I laughed. In this drill that quotation from the poor fool

[81]

Lt. Doob in *Good Soldier Schweik* was really quite in place. Up to now nobody had yet had the courage to use that joke quite so loudly. A distinct poke from my more experienced neighbor in the line told me to stop laughing, that I might be wrong, that it was not meant as a joke. And it wasn't.

The figure whose voice we heard behind us was a tiny creature in an SS uniform, who very evidently had no knowledge of Schweik whatever. It talked like Lt. Doob because it was spiritually related to him. It answered to the name of Withan, and had long served as a top sergeant in the Czechoslovak army under the name of Vitan. He was right, we got to know him quite thoroughly, and we never spoke of him otherwise than in the third person singular—It. To tell the truth, our inventiveness failed when we tried to find a pat nickname for that rich mixture of stupidity, meanness, superiority and plain badness, who was one of the chief pillars of the regime at Pankrats.

"He doesn't reach to a pig's knee," was our expression for those diminutive puffers and climbers when we wished to wound them in the most sensitive spot. How small a person must be mentally to suffer for his small stature. Withan suffered, all right, and took revenge on everybody who was larger physically or mentally—that means on everybody.

Not with blows. He didn't have enough courage for that. But by spying and denouncing. How many prisoners paid with their health for Withan's tattling tales. How many of them paid with their lives—for it makes all the difference in the world what note is written on your card when you leave Pankrats for a concentration camp—or whether you ever get out of Pankrats at all.

He is extremely comical, as he struts down the corridor all alone, greatly impressed with his own importance. He struts even when there is no one to see him. Whenever he meets a person, he feels the need to climb up somewhere. While he is questioning one of us, he sits on the arm of a chair, and can sit there uncomfortably for an hour simply because in that position he is a head taller than you are. When he is on duty while we shave, he stands on a step or parades up and down a bench pronouncing his favorite phrases:

"I don't want to see anything; I don't want to hear anything. You don't know me. . . ."

At morning exercises he takes his position on the little plot of grass which raises him all of four inches higher than the rest of the court-yard. He enters a cell as augustly as your royal majesty, and immediately mounts a chair in order to make his inspection from a suitable elevation.

He is extremely comical, but—like every dunce in public office—extremely dangerous when it comes to human lives. Within his stupidity is hidden one talent—that of making a camel out of a mosquito. He knows nothing but the job of a watch-dog, and therefore any inconsequential deviation from regulations becomes something big, something to match his own self-importance. He construes every infraction of prison rules and orders in a way to cater to his consciousness that he is Somebody. And who is there to investigate how much truth there is to his accusations?

SMETONZ

The hulking figure, dull face and expressionless eyes of Smetonz are the personification of Grosz's cartoons of the Nazi stormtrooper. He was a cow-milker up near the Lithuanian border of East Prussia, but it is queer that the gentle cattle left none of their characteristics on him. Upstairs he is considered the embodiment of German virtues —he is hard, brisk, unbribable. One of the few who does not demand extra food from the trusties whom he passes in the corridor, but. . . .

Some German scientist, I do not recall which, once measured the intelligence of creatures by the number of "words" which they are able to form. On this basis he decided that the domestic cat is the least intelligent of creatures—being able, it seems, to form only 128 "words." Oh, what a genius is the cat compared to Smetonz, from whom Pankrats never heard more than four words:

"Pass bloss auf, Mensch!" "Just look out, you!"

Twice or three times a week he was relieved on duty. Each time he tormented himself, but always bungled the little ceremony hopelessly. I happened to see him when the prison superintendent criticized him for not having any windows open. That mass of flesh rocked back and forth on his stumpy legs, his stupid head leaned a little further forward, the corners of his mouth dropped in the stubborn effort to repeat the order which his ears had just heard . . . and then suddenly that mountain of matter roared like a siren, spreading alarm along all the corridors. Few people knew what it was all about, the windows re-

[84]

mained closed, and two prisoners who happened to be nearest Smetonz began to bleed at the nose. That was his solution.

That is the way he was. He beat whomever he met, beat them even to death. That is all he understood. Nothing else. He entered a cell once and struck one of the occupants. The prisoner, a sick man, fell to the floor in convulsions. Smetonz made all the others do a squatting exercise in time to the poor man's contortions. The cramps died down as the invalid lost strength and became exhausted. And Smetonz placed his hands on his hips with an imbecile smile, as he surveyed his success in solving such a complicated situation.

He was a real primitive, who remembered only one thing out of all they tried to teach him—that beating solved most problems.

Finally something broke even in this creature. It was about a month ago that he and K— were sitting in the reception office of the prison. K— was explaining the situation, explained long and tediously before Smetonz even began to understand. Then he stood up, opened the door of the office, looked carefully down the corridor. Not a sound, the prison slept in the dead of night. He closed the door, carefully locked it and slowly collapsed on a chair:

"Then you think . . .?"

He rested his chin in his hand. A terrible burden settled on the tiny soul in that huge body. Long he sat before raising his head and saying hopelessly:

"You are right. We can't win. . . ."

For the past month Pankrats has not head the war-cry

of Smetonz. The new prisoners do not know the weight of his fist.

THE PRISON DIRECTOR

A small *Untersturmführer*, sub-platoon leader, always elegantly dressed, whether in uniform or not, prosperous-looking, he was very satisfied with himself. He was a lover of dogs, the hunt and of women—but that is a matter which does not concern us.

The other sides of his character—which do concern Pankrats—are his coarseness, his unlettered roughness. A typical Nazi upstart, willing to sacrifice anybody to hold his own position. He came from Poland and is named Soppa, if the name means anything. They say he was an apprentice blacksmith, but that honest trade left no marks on him. It was long ago that he entered Hitler's service and won his present position by flattery and intrigue. He protects his job with every possible trick. He is without regard or feeling for any of the prisoners or his own staff, for children or for elders. There is not much feeling for Nazism among the personnel of Pankrats, but none of them is quite so completely without a shadow of feeling as Soppa. The only man whom he values at all, with whom he often talks, is the prison medic, police-master Weisner. But the relation does not seem to be mutual.

Soppa thinks only of himself. He earned his ruling position only for himself, and only for himself will he remain loyal to the regime till the last moment. He is about the only one who ever considers some other means of salvation,

[86]

but now knows that there is none. The fall of Nazism will be his own fall, will put an end to his prosperous life, to his splendid apartment, an end to his own elegance—which has never hesitated to make use of the clothes of executed Czechs.

Yes, that will be the end of him.

THE PRISON MEDIC

Policemaster Weisner—what a peculiar figure on the Pankrats stage. You often feel that he is out of place here— but then you can't imagine Pankrats without him. When he is not in the infirmary, you find him gliding down the corridors with his short, rocking steps—talking to himself and observing everything about him, always observing. He is like some foreigner who wandered in here and wished to carry away with him the most possible details. But he is able to stick a key in a lock and open a cell as quietly and fast as any stool pigeon. He has a dry humor which permits him to say things with hidden meanings, but without giving away anything on which you can trip him up. He makes up to people, but never permits anyone to make up to him. He sees a great deal, but does not carry tales and does not accuse others. If he enters a cell full of smoke, he sniffs audibly and says:

"Well," and smacks his lips, "there is smoking in the cells." Smacks his lips again and says, "Strictly forbidden."

But he won't report it. His face is always wrinkled and worried, as though some great torment were troubling him. It is apparent he wishes to have nothing to do with the regime he serves, and whose victims he cares for all day. He does not believe in this regime, does not believe it will be permanent, and never did believe it. That is why he did not move his family from Breslau to Prague, although very few of the officials from the Reich passed up that opportunity to gorge in an occupied country. But he is equally incapable of having anything in common with the people who struggle against the regime. He does not lean to either side.

He took care of me dutifully and honestly. He does so with most of his patients, and often stubbornly forbids prisoners who have been tortured too much to be carted down for further grilling. Perhaps that quiets his conscience. Sometimes, however, he refuses his help where it is most needed. Perhaps when he is gripped with fear.

He is a typical little citizen, standing alone between his fear of the powers that be and his fear of what will happen next. He looks everywhere for a solution, but finds none. Not a rat, but a real little mouse caught in a trap.

Hopelessly caught.

"FLINK"

This one is not a mere figurine, nor yet a whole character. Something between the two. He has not the clear perception needed to make him a personality.

There are two of that sort here: simple people, passively sensitive, merely terrified at first by the horrors into which they have stumbled, then longing to find a way out of them. They search for any sort of mental support, for they are not self-reliant men. They search for support by intuition rather than by perception. They help you merely in the hope of receiving help from you. It is right to give them help—both now and in the future.

These two are also the only two of all the German officials in Pankrats who have been at the front.

Hanauer was a tailor from Znojmo, who returned early from the eastern front with frostbite, which he himself arranged. "Warfare is not for people," he philosophizes in Schweik style. "Nothing in it for me."

Höfer, a cheerful shoemaker from the Bata Works, went through the French campaign and then deserted his military duty, even though he had a promotion promised. "Oh, sh—!" was his expression as he waved his hand over all the complications he got into daily—and they were plenty.

These two were very much alike in their feelings and their fate. But Höfer was the more fearless, the more expressive, the more complete personality of the two. Flink is the nickname for him in almost all the cells.

The day he is on duty is a day of calm in the cells. Do whatever you wish. If he shouts at you, he winks his eye to show that he doesn't mean you, but that the inspector down below must hear how stern he is in action. His efforts at severity are wasted, however. He no longer convinces anyone, and no week goes by without his being punished.

"Oh, sh—!" He waves his hand and goes his own way. He is still a young frivolous shoemaker's helper, rather than a guard. You can catch him playing pennies against the wall cheerfully, even passionately, with the boys in the cells. A moment later he will drive the prisoners out into the corridor to inspect the cell. If the inspection lasts too long and you get curious, you will find him sitting at the table, his head on his arms, asleep. Calmly and luxuriously sleeping. He is safe here from his superiors because the prisoners in the corridors keep watch and warn him of any approaching danger. He needs to sleep while on duty, for his rest at night is disturbed by the girl whom he loves above everything in the world.

Will Nazism be victorious or defeated? "Oh, sh—! Do you think it possible that this circus go on for ever?"

He does not count himself among them. That makes him interesting. What is more, he does not wish to belong to them, and doesn't belong to them. If you need to deliver a secret note to some other department, Flink will take care of it. If you need to send word to someone outside, Flink will take it out. If you need to talk with someone in order to convince him and thus save the lives of further people, Flink will take you to his cell and stand watch outside—proud as street boy of his ability to put one over on the police. You often have to argue with him to be careful—in the midst of danger he does not feel it much. He is not at all conscious of the true significance of the good he does. It just relieves him to do as much as he can, but that interferes with his real growth.

He is not yet a personality, but is growing into one.

"KOLIN"

It was one evening in Martial Law. The guard in SS uniform who let me into the cell went through my pockets very superficially.

"How are you getting along?" he asked in a whisper.

"I don't know. They told me I'll be shot tomorrow."

"Did that terrify you?"

"I've been expecting it."

For a moment he ran his hands mechanically down my coat lapels.

"Maybe they will do it. Perhaps not tomorrow; perhaps sometime; perhaps not at all. But in times like these . . . it is well to be prepared. . . ."

Then he was silent.

"But in case they should, would you like to send word to someone? Or . . . would you like to write? Not for present publication, you understand, but for the future. How you got in here, whether anyone betrayed you, how certain ones behaved. Just so what you know doesn't pass out with you."

Would I like to write? As though that weren't my most fervent desire!

In a moment he had brought paper and pencil; I hid them carefully so that no inspection should discover them.

But I never touched them for a long time.

It was too good to be true—I couldn't believe it. Too wonderful in this dark building, a few weeks after being arrested, to find a man in the uniform of those who only shouted and beat you—to find a man. To find a friend who gives you his hand, and helps you to speak for at least a moment with those who will outlive all this—and even with those who will not outlive it. And at the very moment when they are calling out names of those to be executed, in the midst of men drunk with blood, and among those whose throats choke with terror so that they could not cry out if they wished. To find a friend at such a moment—no, that is unbelievable. If it isn't true, then it is at least a warning. But what strength of spirit a man must have to put out his hand of his own accord to a person in a situation like mine! What courage!

About a month passed. Martial law had been repealed, the shouting died down, the cruelest hours had turned to memories. It was evening, and again I returned from a grilling with the same guard to let me into the cell.

"I see you pulled through. Was everything all right?" He looked very solicitous.

I knew what he meant, and that question moved me deeply. It also convinced me more than anything else of his sincerity. Only a man who had the moral right to ask that question could ever have asked it. From that moment I believed him; he was one of us.

He was a strange person at first sight. He walked the corridors alone—a calm, close-mouthed man, cautious and observing. You never heard him shout. You never saw him strike anyone.

"The next time Smetonz looks this way hit me one, please." My neighbors in the other cell were asking him to be a little more active for his own sake.

"That isn't necessary," he said, shaking his head.

You never heard him speak anything but Czech. Everything about him told you that he was different from all the rest, but you would have had a hard time to say why. They also felt it, but weren't able to put their finger on the reason.

He succeeds in being everywhere he is needed. He brings calm where people have become excited and confused. He brings encouragement where people hang their heads. He makes a new contact where more lives outside are threatened and our connection has been broken with the people who can save them. He doesn't get buried in details, but works systematically and on a broad scale.

This is nothing new. We went into Nazi service from the beginning with this in mind.

Adolf Kolinsky, the Czech guard we are talking about, from an old Czech family in Moravia, pretended to be a German in applying for a job guarding Czech prisoners first in Hradec Kralove and then in Pankrats. There must have been bitter thoughts among those who knew him. Four years later the German prison superintendent waves his fist in Kolinsky's face and threatens:

"I'll drive that Czechishness out of you!"

A little late in the game. And the superintendent is mistaken. He would have to transform not only Kolinsky's Czechness, but crush the very humanity in him. Here is a man who consciously and voluntarily signed up with the enemy in order to fight him within his own ranks, and to help others fight him. A man whom constant danger has only strengthened in his purpose.

OURS

If they had brought us cocoa for breakfast on February 11, 1943, instead of the black brew made of I don't know what, we would hardly have noticed that miracle. Because that morning another miracle happened—the uniform of a Czech policeman hovered around our cell.

It only hovered. All we saw was one step of the black trousers and high boots. A dark blue sleeve and a hand lifted to the lock, opened and then closed the cell door, and disappeared. It all happened so fast that a quarter hour later we were ready to believe that we had never seen it.

A Czech policeman in Pankrats! What ramifying conclusions one could draw from that one fact:

Within two hours we were drawing them. The door of the cell opened again and a Czech police cap looked in and lips said, smiling broadly at our surprise:

"*Freistunde!*" "Recess!"

There could be no mistake now. Among the green-gray uniforms of the SS guards in the corridors, there had appeared several dark spots—Czech police officers—who looked very radiant to us.

What could this mean for us? What sort will they be? But whatever sort they are, the very fact that they are here speaks pretty plain language. How near to the end must a regime be when it must accept into its most sensitive apparatus, into the most important organization it has for support, members of the very nation which it wishes to oppress? What an extreme lack of manpower it must suffer at the front, if it is willing to weaken its police power just to gain a few individual soldiers! How long do you suppose that regime hopes to last at this rate?

Of course they would send only selected men here, who may turn out worse than the German guards, who have lost their alertness and their faith in victory. But the fact, the very fact that Czech police are substituted for SS men is an unassailable proof that the end is near.

That is the way we argued.

And there were many more of them than we allowed ourselves to suppose at first. The fact was that the machine had very little choice, there simply were not men enough for all the work the regime had to do to protect itself.

We first saw Czech uniforms in Pankrats on February 11.

The next day we began to get acquainted with the men in them.

One would come along, look into the cell, shifting feet uneasily on the threshold. Then answer our look with sudden courage, like a little kid which jumps up on all fours with one burst of peevish energy.

"Well, how are we getting along, gentlemen?"

We reply with a smile, and he smiles back. Then bursts out with:

"Don't be angry with us. Believe me, we would rather go on tramping the pavement outside there than watch you in here. We had to do it, but perhaps—perhaps something good will come of it. . . ."

He was happy when we told him what we thought of their coming into Pankrats, and what we thought of them. Thus we became friends from the first moment. That was Vitek, a simple goodhearted boy—the first one who hovered around the door of our cell that first morning.

The second was Tuma, a really typical old Czech cop. Rough and noisy but fundamentally good—the sort we used to call "Pop" in the jails of the Republic. He saw nothing

[95]

exceptional in his position. On the contrary, he felt right at home and maintained order, or broke it, in his own way with the usual coarse jokes. He would hand some bread into the cell, or cigarettes, pass the time in conversation with anybody about anything, except the political situation. He did it all perfectly naturally, not hiding the fact that this was his conception of guard duty. The first reproof he received for it made him more careful, but did not change him. He was still old Pop, the cop. You would never dare ask anything big of him, but you breathed easier with him around.

The third Czech policeman paced the corridors scowling, speechless, seeing nothing. Paid no attention to attempts to approach him.

"They didn't get much when they chose that one," said Daddy after watching him a week. "He is the least successful of them all."

"Or else the smartest," said I, for the sake of argument, since opposing views on small matters are the spice of life in a cell.

Two weeks later it seemed to me that the silent one winked an eye slightly out of the line of duty. I replied with the same signal, which can have a thousand meanings in prison. But nothing happened; I was probably mistaken.

A month later, however, everything came clear. It came suddenly like a butterfly breaking its cocoon. The scowling cocoon cracked and a living being appeared. It was not a butterfly, but a man.

"You are building monuments," said Daddy about several of these character sketches.

[96]

That I would like to do, in order to keep alive the memory of comrades who fought truly and bravely here and outside, and who fell. But I would like also to memorialize the living who helped us no less faithfully and no less courageously in the most difficult conditions. I should like to bring personalities like Kolinsky and this Czech policeman out of the ghostly corridors of Pankrats into the light of life. Not for their glory, but as an example to others. Because human duty will not end with this battle, and it will require heroism to be men as long as people are not truly human.

The story of policeman Jaroslav Hora is a very brief story. But in it one finds the life story of a whole man.

Radnicko is a far corner of the country, in a beautiful region, but dreary and poor. His father was a glassmaker, who led a hard life. Drudgery when there was work, and poverty when unemployment made its home in the land. That either threw one to his knees or raised one's head in dreams of a better world. To believe in a better world and fight for it, his father became a Communist.

Young Jarda rode among the bicycle troop in the May Day parade with a red ribbon woven round the wheels. He did not leave that red ribbon there, but carried it somewhere inside him when he went to work in the lathe shop, to his first job with Skoda Works.

The unemployment crisis came, then military service, then a chance for a job with the police. I don't know what the red ribbon in him was doing all that time—perhaps it was rolled up and laid away somewhere, perhaps half forgotten—but not lost. One day they assigned him to duty in

Pankrats. He did not come voluntarily, like Kolinsky, with a purpose already worked out. But he became conscious of a purpose the first time he looked into a cell. The ribbon unrolled.

First he had to scout out the field of action and measure his own strength. His face scowled with concentrated thought, where to begin and how to begin. He was no professional politician, but a simple son of the people. He had the experience of his father, however, a firm kernel of character around which his decision formed. When he was decided what to do, a man broke out of his scowling cocoon.

He was a fine person inside, remarkably clean, sensitive, shy but manly. He dared whatever was necessary. Both small and large things are necessary, so he does small things and large. He works quietly, without gesticulating, deliberately, but without fear. It is all so natural to him, the categorical imperative within him. This is what has to be done, so why talk about it?

That is about all. That is the whole story of one character, who today can count to his credit several human lives saved. Those people still live and work outside because one man in Pankrats did his human duty. He does not know them personally, nor they him. Nor do they know Kolinsky, but I hope they will get acquainted afterwards. These two workers found each other very quickly, and made the best use of their opportunities for service.

Remember their example. The example of two men who had their heads with them and their hearts in the right place, and made full use of both.

DAD SKOREPA

When by chance you see all three together, you have a living picture of fraternization—the gray-green uniform of the SS guard Kolinsky, the dark blue uniform of the Czech police, Hora, and the light, unhappy uniform of the prison trusty, Dad Skorepa. You see them together very rarely, however—very rarely. For the simple reason that they belong together.

Prison regulations allow work in the corridors, cleaning and serving meals, to be done "only by particularly reliable prisoners, disciplined and strictly isolated from the others." That is the letter of the law, the dead letter—woefully dead. There are no such trusties, and never have been. Certainly not in any Gestapo prisons. The trusties here are antennae, feelers thrust out by the prison collective in the cells to contact the free world in order to live and communicate with others. How many trusties have paid with their lives for some message which was intercepted, for being caught with a secret note on them! But the law of the prison collective mercilessly demands of their successors that they continue the same dangerous work. Whether they go into it courageously or are afraid—they are forced to work for the collective. One only risks more if one is afraid, only loses out sooner or later, as in all underground work.

This is underground work of the nth degree, directly under the hands of those who are set to stamp out opposition. In the sight of guards, in posts which they assign, under a rigid schedule set by the enemy—under most difficult conditions. Everything you have learned about illegal work outside is inadequate here, but you are required to do as much or more than before.

There are masters of illegal work outside, and masters of it here among the trusties. Dad Skorepa is a past master, quiet and unassuming in appearance, but as agile as a fish. The guards praise him—look what a drudge, how dependable, interested only in doing his duty, far from anything which is against regulations. They tell other trusties to follow his example!

Yes, trusties, follow his example! He is really a paragon of trusties as prisoners wish them, the sturdiest and yet most sensitive of the collective's antennae.

He knows who is in every cell, knows every newcomer from the first moment—why he is here, who his contacts are, how he has behaved outside and how his pals have behaved. He makes a study of "cases" and tries to unravel them all. That is important if he wishes to carry through outside contacts and occasionally to give sound advice.

He knows the enemy, also. Makes a careful study of each guard, his habits, his strong and weak points, what to watch out for in him, what he can be used for, how to trick him or put him off the track. Many of the guards' characteristics which I have used were told me by Dad Skorepa. He knows them all, can define them exactly and well. That is important to one who wishes to move freely about the corridors and do his work effectively.

But above all, Skorepa knows his own duty. He is a Communist who knows that he must be a Communist every moment, that there is no time or place to fold his hands in his lap and "let the work ride." I should say that he has found his best place here in the greatest danger and under the heaviest pressure. He has even grown while here.

He is elastic; each day or hour presents new situations which demand new methods. He invents them fast and cleverly. He may have only a fraction of a minute. That is enough to knock on a cell door, listen through the peep-hole to a carefully prepared message and then deliver it clearly and exactly to a cell at the other end of the corridor between the moment that his guard goes down stairs and the relief comes up one flight of stairs. He is careful and has great presence of mind. Hundreds of prison notes have gone through his hands—not one was caught, nor even suspected.

He knows instinctively who is in trouble, who needs encouragement with a few words on the situation outside. He knows whom he can encourage with a special look of those fatherly eyes of his, when a man needs strength to fight down despair. He knows who needs an extra roll or ladle of soup to build up strength for the next period of hunger punishment. He knows such things from thorough experience and his own tender feelings—and then does what is necessary in each case.

That is Dad Skorepa. A soldier, strong and fearless. A real man.

I should like those of you who will read this someday to see in him, not only one man, but the best type of trusty, *Hausarbeiter,* who has been able to transform the work demanded of them by the oppressor into service to the oppressed. There is only one Dad Skorepa here, but there are others of different human cast who also serve

[101]

the cause, and serve no less than he. I wished to sketch them all, here in Pankrats and those in Petchek building, but am sorry there are only a few hours left—too short for "the song which is sung so briefly, but is lived so long."

So there is time only for a few more names, a few examples of the many, whom it is but fair to remember:

"Renek"—Josef Teringl is a hard, inflammable, sacrificial man connected with quite a lot of the history of Petchek Building and our struggle in it. As is his inseparable good-hearted pal, Joe Bervidu.

Dr. Milosh Nedved, a handsome and noble boy, who paid for his daily assistance to our imprisoned comrades with his life at Oswiecim.

Arnost Lorenz, whose wife was executed because he refused to betray his comrades. A man who went to his death a year later in order to save his friends, the trusties of Number 400 and their whole collective.

Vashek Rezku, of wonderful, indestructible humor.

Anny Vikova, close-mouthed and deeply devoted, who was executed during Martial Law.

Springer, that clever, ever cheerful "librarian," who always invented new ways to do his necessary work.

Bilek, that tender youth. . . .

These are merely examples, samples. Personalities, great or small, but always real characters—never mere figures.

Chapter VIII

A BIT OF HISTORY

June 9th, 1943.

In front of my cell there hangs a belt. My belt. The sign of a transport in the near future. Some time in the night they will take me off to the Reich for trial—and so forth. From the last crust of my life, time bites off the final mouthful. The four hundred and eleven days in Pankrats have passed surprisingly fast. How many days remain? What sort of days? And where will I spend them?

I shall hardly have the opportunity to write, however, anywhere else. So this is my last testimony. A bit of history, of which I am apparently the last living witness.

In February, 1941, they arrested the whole Central Committee of the Communist Party in Czechoslovakia—and also the second group of leaders, who had prepared to take over when we should fall. How it happened that such an extremely hard blow fell on us all at once has never been fully explained. Perhaps it will be explained some day, when the Gestapo commissars are caught and made to talk. I tried in vain to learn that secret as a trusty in Petchek Building. There was certainly some spy-work in it, and a lot of carelessness. Two years of successful work underground had dulled the alertness of the comrades. Our illegal organization grew too widespread; new workers were constantly drawn in—even many who ought to have been held in reserve to succeed the first set if anything happened. Our network of cells became too complex to control precisely. The blow at our party Central was evidently prepared long and carefully, and fell just when the enemy was ready for his attack on the Soviet Union.

I did not know at first how many of us they had trapped. I waited for the rest to contact me according to the normal plan, but I waited in vain. After a month, it was plain to see that something pretty far-reaching had happened, and that I must not merely wait for a contact from outside. Thus I began to look for contacts from inside, and others began the search also.

The first member whom I found was Honza Vyskochil, chief of the Central Bohemia section. He had plenty of initiative and already had some material ready to renew publication of *Red Rights,* so that the party should not be left without a newspaper. I wrote a leading editorial, but then we agreed that the material, the rest of which I had not yet seen, should be published as a *May Paper,* not under the name of *Red Rights.* Other parties had put out similar one-shot papers instead of trying to maintain regular editions.

The next months were devoted to partisan work. The blow, severe as it was, could not kill the party. Hundreds of new workers took up the tasks left by leaders who had been struck down. Their fresh energy and devotion prevented any deterioration in the basic organization or any feeling of defeatism or passivity creeping into it. But the central organism was missing, and the danger of partisan

[104]

group work was that there would not be unity and well-knit leadership at the most important moment, the expected assault of the enemy on Soviet Russia.

I saw that an experienced political hand was at work in a copy of *Red Rights,* which was published by a partisan cell. Our single *May Paper* was not particularly successful, I am sorry to say, but others saw in it proof that there was someone to cooperate with. So we two groups searched for contact.

It was like looking for someone in a deep forest. We would hear a voice and start out to find it. Then the right voice sounded ever so quietly from an entirely different direction. Our heavy losses made everybody in the party extremely cautious and alert to prevent falling into a trap. Two members of the former Central who wished to find each other had to pass through all sorts of tests and overcome many obstacles set up by those they trusted in order to make doubly sure that neither had turned traitor and was trying to play a trick. The greatest handicap was that I did not know who it was I was looking for—nor did he know the member was trying to contact him.

We finally found a man who knew and could vouch for us both. That was a fine young fellow, Dr. Milosh Nedved, who became our first courier. I found him by pure chance. In the middle of June, 1941, I fell ill and sent Lida to find Dr. Nedved and bring him to the Baxa home, where I was hiding. He came at once, and in our talk he let me know very, very cautiously that he had been asked to find the fellow who wrote that editorial in *May Paper.* He had no suspicion that it was I, for all the members on the other side were sure that I had been arrested and probably executed.

Hitler attacked the Soviet Union on June 22, 1941. That very evening Honza Vyskochil and I put out a leaflet showing what that meant for us in Czechoslovakia. On June 30 I finally met the man I had been looking for so long. He came to the address which I indicated because he knew whom he was to meet. I did not yet know who he was. It was a summer night, the acacias perfumed the air, a night for a lovers' tryst. Before either spoke, we covered the window. When I lit the light, we embraced each other. It was Honza Zika.

In February, 1941, the whole Central Committee was not yet arrested. One lone member was still at large, Zika. I had known him a long time and liked him immensely. But only now did we come to know each other well, in the work we took up together. He was short and roundish, constantly smiling, a fine uncle of a man—but devoted and decisive, hard and uncompromising in party work. He did not know, and did not wish to know anything except the work he was supposed to do. He denied himself everything in order to do his duty. He loved people, and people loved him. But he never bought a soul by winking at their short-comings.

It only took a few minutes to come to agreement. And within a few days I knew a third member of the new leadership, with whom Zika had been in contact since May, Honza Cherny. He was a strapping elegant chap with a wonderful attitude to people. He had fought in Spain, from where he had come home after the war broke out, crossing

Nazi Germany with a lung wound. He always remained something of a soldier, with a rich underground experience, talented, always taking the initiative.

Months of stubborn fighting made us excellent comrades. We seemed to complement each other well, both in temperament and in our special training. Zika was the organizer, realistic, vexingly precise, never misled by high-sounding phrases. He bored into every report until he knew its full significance, tested every proposal from every possible side and then kindly, but firmly, carried out every decision of the group.

Cherny was in charge of sabotage and preparations for armed revolt. He thought in military language, was inventive, planned in broad terms, on a grand scale, was tireless and successful in searching for new people and new resources.

I was the journalist, the political agitator, relying on my nose. A little fantastic at times, a stickler for balance and unity.

Our division of functions was a division of responsibility, not of work. We all had to take a hand and accept responsibility in each other's branches whenever independent action or decision was called for, since it was hard to meet and discuss everything. The blow which struck the party in February, had cut all our contacts and they could never be entirely repaired. Certain whole sections of the organization had been crushed; others had been rebuilt, but it proved impossible to contact them. The cells in many factories, even the organization in whole regions, worked in isolation for months before we could communicate with them. We could only hope that they received our central newspaper and count on their following the general line it indicated.

It was hard to work, when we did not even have places to live. We could not use former apartments because they were probably under constant watch by the enemy. At first we had no money, even, and it was hard to secure food without ration cards, which would have given away our identity. All these obstacles had to be overcome at a time when it was too late to prepare and build, when we had to take an active hand in the battle, for the Soviet Union had been attacked.

It is our job to fight on the internal front against the invaders, fight the miniature battles of sabotage. Not with our own forces only, but so far as possible to bring to bear the strength of the whole Czech nation. During the preparatory years from 1939 to 1941 the party was in underground activity, not only against the German police, but in relation to the nation. In spite of bloody suppression, the party had to harden and perfect its organization against the invaders and at the same time win the confidence of the nation. That meant approaching people who belonged to no party, dealing with anyone who was determined to fight for liberty, calling upon the whole people to struggle, and dealing directly with those who continued to hesitate.

By the beginning of September, 1941, we could not say that we had rebuilt our crippled organization, but we could say that we had at least a firmly organized core, capable of taking on considerable tasks. Party campaigns began to attract attention. Sabotage spread, there were strikes in factories everywhere. At the end of September they sent Heydrich after us.

The first period of martial law did not break our increasingly active resistance. It did slow us down, however, and inflicted new wounds on the party. The worst hit were the Prague district and youth organization. More of our leaders fell, so valuable to the party—Jan Kreychi, Shtanzl, Milosh Krasny, and many others.

After each blow, however, you saw how indestructible the party was. Even if he seemed irreplacable, each worker who fell was replaced by two or three new ones. By the new year we again had a strong organization built. If it was not as far-reaching as that we had in February, 1941, still it was fully capable of meeting the challenge to decisive battle. We all took a hand in the work, but the major credit goes to Honza Zika.

Proofs of our publication work are to be found in attics and cellars, in the hidden files of comrades, and it is unnecessary to speak of that here.

Our newspapers were widely circulated and read, not only by members of the party, but throughout the land. They were published in printed or mimeographed form in considerable numbers by many "technical centers," all secret and strictly isolated from each other. No publishing group knew who worked in any other, nor where they worked. None knew where their instructions or articles came from. They all worked as fast as humanly possible, as the battle situation demanded. For instance we put out the Army General Order of Comrade Stalin of February 23, 1942, and had it in the hands of readers on the evening of the 24th. The printers worked splendidly, as did the technical group of doctors and that called Fuchs-Lorenz, which also issued its own paper named *The World Against Hitler*. Most of the material of the other papers I produced myself, so as not to endanger others. My substitute was prepared long in advance in case I should fall. He took over immediately I was arrested, and is still doing his job.

We built as simple a machine as we could, to involve as few people as possible in any one task. We dropped the system of complicated chains for delivering messages, which did not save the committee in February, 1941, but actually increased the danger of betrayal. That left each of us more exposed individually, but put the whole apparatus in a safer position. No future blow could cripple the party again, as happened in February.

Thus the Central Committee continued working normally when I was arrested. My substitute stepped into my place and even my closest collaborators noticed no difference.

Honza Zika was arrested on the night of May 27, 1942. That was also by pure chance. It was the night after the assassination of Heydrich, when the whole enemy machine was afoot conducting raids all over Prague. They walked into the apartment in Streshovice, where Zika lived illegally. His documents were in order with a false name, and they might never have noticed him if he had kept calm. Not wishing to risk the lives of the good family who had sheltered him, however, he tried to escape from a second-story window. He fell, mortally injured his spine and was taken to a prison hospital. They had no idea whom they had laid hands on. Only after eighteen days of search and comparison of files of photographs, did they prove who he was and took him dying to Petchek Building for a grilling. We met there for the last time, when they led me in to see him. We shook hands, and he beamed that broad kind smile at me, saying:

"Take care of yourself, Julo!"

That was all they ever heard out of him. He never said another word to them. After a few blows in the face he fainted, and died in a couple of hours.

I had learned of his arrest by May 29. Our feelers were working well. Through them we had agreed on our next steps as best we could, and they were later approved by Honza Cherny. That was our last decision together for the party.

Honza Cherny was arrested in the summer of 1942. This time it was not by chance, but due to a flagrant breach of discipline by Jan Pokorny, who had direct contact with him. Pokorny did not behave like a responsible officer of the group. After several hours of grilling—pretty severe grilling, to be sure, but what else had he expected?—after several hours of grilling he grew panicky and told them the address of the apartment where he had met Cherny. From there they traced Honza, and Gestapo had him a few days later.

They dragged me in to identify him the moment they brought him in.

"Do you know him?"

"No, I don't."

Nor did he admit knowing me. He refused to answer any more questions whatever. His old wound saved him from long torture. He soon fainted. Before they could take him for a second grilling, we carefully informed him about the situation and he was guided accordingly.

They never got anything out of him. They held him in prison a long time, waiting for some new evidence to break down his silence. But they never broke Honza Cherny.

Imprisonment did not change him. He was always courageous, sprightly, cheerful—always pointing others into the future, when his own future pointed straight toward death.

They took him away from Pankrats suddenly, the end of April. I don't know where. This sudden disappearance of people from here always means something ominous. I may be wrong, but I never expect to see Honza Cherny again.

We always reckoned with death. We knew that falling into Gestapo hands meant the end. And we acted accordingly, both in our own souls and in relation to others, even after being caught.

My own play draws near its end. I can't write that end, for I don't yet know what it will be. This is no longer a play. This is life.

In real life there are no spectators: you all participate in life.

The curtain rises on the last act.

I loved you all, friends. Be on guard!

JULIUS FUCHIK.

June 9, 1943.